Health Education
and
Training in Schools and Colleges

Health Education
and
Training in Schools and Colleges

George K. Mathews

CRESCENT
PUBLISHING CORPORATION

[The responsibility for the facts stated, conclusions reached and plagiarism, if any, in this book is entirely that of the Author. And the Publisher bears no responsibility for them, whatsoever.]

Health Education and Training in Schools and Colleges

First Published : 2009

ISBN 978-81-8342-124-9

Published by :

CRESCENT PUBLISHING CORPORATION
4831/24, Prahlad Street,
Ansari Road, Darya Ganj,
New Delhi - 110002
Ph. : 23272541, 23257835
Fax : 91- 011- 23257835
e-mail : campusbooks@hotmail.com

Printed at :
Roshan Offset Printers
Delhi

Preface

Health as a whole, consisting of physical, mental and social wellbeing, can lead to a better quality of life. The aim of health and physical education is to enable all students to enhance their quality of life through active living. Participation in sports influences health by training and developing the body. By education students are to become more conscious of the importance of their own lifestyles in respect of health and environment, and to develop an awareness of their bodies, and a positive self image. Students are to gain increased knowledge about food, exercise and ergonomics as well as the harmful effects of drugs and doping.

This book is designed to give students the opportunity of trying out different physical activities that are coupled with their own experience and interests. Students are to broaden their knowledge in the areas of sport and health, and gain the knowledge needed to be able to reflect independently over, and analyse ways and methods of, achieving health and wellbeing, both from an individual viewpoint as well as that of a civic perspective.

The book will lead to students to find different ways of conducting individual physical training, and develop and strengthen their health, both whilst at school, and later during further studies and working life.

George K. Mathews

Contents

1

Importance of Health Education and Training

The Ottawa Charter was forged only 8 years after the historic Alma Ata meeting, which had declared Health for All by 2000. With hindsight, the goal of shaping a new and healthier world was already in jeopardy. Perhaps, aware of this nascent weakening of the prospects for population health, the global health promotion community called for the revitalisation of ambitious large-scale thinking. New strategies were devised to energise healthy individual and community behaviours, reflected in phrases such as 'healthy choices should be easy choices' and 'healthy public policy'.

Nevertheless, over the ensuing two decades, the adverse social, economic and environmental trends that were already beginning to jeopardise, Health for All in 1986 have strengthened. Further, economic globalisation, with increasingly powerful transnational companies shaping global consumer behaviours, has tended to make unhealthy choices the easier choices, including cigarettes, fast-food diets, high-sugar drinks, automated domestic technologies and others. These changes have occurred despite an increased understanding of the fundamental determinants of population health. Some of these foundations of health are at risk, and in some regions, hard-won health gains have recently been reversed. Recent attempts to re-focus attention on global public goods, such as in the Millennium Development Goals (MDGs), are weak in comparison to the scale of today's problems.

There is an urgent strategic need for health promotion to engage with the international discourse on 'sustainability'. To date much of the discussion and policy development addressing 'sustainable development' has treated the economy, livelihoods, energy supplies, urban infrastructure, food-producing ecosystems, wilderness conservation and convivial communal living as if they were ends in themselves: the goals of sustainability. Clearly, those are all major assets that value. But their value inheres in their being the foundations upon which the health and survival of populations depend. The ultimate goal of sustainability is to ensure human well-being, health and survival. If our way of living, of managing the natural environment and of organising economic and social relations between people, groups and cultures does not maintain the flows of food and materials, freshwater supplies, environmental stability and other prerequisites for health, then that is a non-sustainable state.

Lacking space to be comprehensive, focus upon infectious diseases, the decline in life expectancy in several regions, the increasingly ominous challenge of large-scale environmental change and how globalisation, trade and economic policy relate to indices of public health. Other emerging health issues not discussed here also reflect major recent shifts in human ecology. They too pose great environmental or social risks to health. They include urbanisation, population ageing, the breakdown of traditional culture and relations and the worldwide move towards a more affluent diet and its associated environmentally damaging food production methods.

There are two fundamental causes for the selected emerging health risks. First, most important, is the global dominance of economic policies which accord primacy to market forces, liberalised trade and the associated intensification of material throughput at the expense of other aspects of social, environmental and personal well-being. For millions in the emerging global middle class, materialism and consumerism have increased at the expense of social relations and leisure time. The gap between rich and poor, both domestically and internationally, has increased substantially in recent decades. Inequality between countries has weakened the United Nations and other global institutions. Foreign aid has declined, replaced by claims that market forces will reduce poverty and provide public goods, including health care and environmental stability.

The second fundamental threat to the improvement and maintenance of population health is the recent advent of unprecedented global environmental changes. The scale of the human enterprise is now such that we are collectively exceeding the capacity of the planet to supply, replenish and absorb. Stocks of accessible oil appear to be declining. Meanwhile, the global emissions of carbon dioxide from fossil fuel combustion, and of other greenhouse gases from industrial and agricultural activities, are rapidly and now dangerously altering the global climate. Worldwide, land degradation, fisheries depletion, freshwater shortages and biodiversity losses are all increasing. The human population, now exceeding 6500 million, continues to increase by over 70 million persons per annum. The number of chronically undernourished people (over 800 million) is again increasing, after gradual declines in the 1980s and early 1990s. Famines in Africa remain frequent, and 300 million undernourished people live in India alone. Meanwhile, hundreds of millions of people are overnourished and, particularly via obesity, will incur an increasing burden of chronic diseases, especially diabetes and heart disease.

The scale of these health risks is unprecedented. The global food crises of the 1960s were averted by the subsequent Green Revolution. Today, a broader-based revolution is required, not only to increase food production, but also to promote peace and international cooperation, slow climate change, ensure environmental protection, eliminate hunger and extreme poverty, quell resurgent infectious diseases and neutralise the obesogenic environment. This enormous population health task goes well beyond that envisaged by the MDGs.

It is, of course, difficult to get an accurate measure of these emerging risks to health. Some, such as climate change, future food suffi-ciency and the threat from weapons of mass destruction, may prove soluble. However, because of the inevitable time lag in understanding, evaluating and responding to these complex problems, the health promotion community should now take serious account of them. There is an expanding peer-reviewed literature on these several emerging problem, areas. To constrain health promotion by sidestepping them would be to risk being 'penny wise but pound foolish'.

Emerging and Re-emerging Infectious Diseases

In the early 1970s, it was widely assumed that infectious diseases would continue to decline: sanitation, vaccines and antibiotics were at hand. The subsequent generalised upturn in infectious diseases was unexpected. Worldwide, at least 30 new and re-emerging infectious diseases have been recognised since 1975. HIV/AIDS has become a serious pandemic.

Several 'old' infectious diseases, including tuberculosis, malaria, cholera and dengue fever, have proven unexpectedly problematic, because of increased antimicrobial resistance, new ecological niches, weak public health services and activation of infectious agents (e.g. tuberculosis) in people whose immune system is weakened by AIDS. Diarrhoeal disease, acute respiratory infections and other infections continue to kill more than seven million infants and children annually. Mortality rates among children are increasing in parts of sub-Saharan Africa.

The recent upturn in the range, burden and risk of infectious diseases reflects a general increase in opportunities for entry into the human species, transmission and long-distance spread, including by air travel. Although specific new infectious diseases cannot be predicted, understanding of the conditions favouring disease emergence and spread is improving. Influences include increased population density, increasingly vulnerable population age distributions and persistent poverty.

Many environmental, political and social factors contribute. These include increasing encroachment upon exotic ecosystems and disturbance of various internal biotic controls among natural ecosystems. There are ampli-fied opportunities for viral mixing, such as in 'wet animal markets'. Industrialised livestock farming also facilitates infections (such as avian influensa) emerging and spreading, and perhaps to increase in virulence. Both under- and over-nutrition and impaired immunity (including in people with poorly controlled diabetes-an obesity-associated disease now increasing globally) contribute to the persistence and spread of infectious diseases. Large-scale human-induced environmental change, including climate change, is of increasing importance.

These causes of infectious disease emergence and spread are compounded by gender, economic and structural inequities, by political ignorance and denial (particularly obvious with HIV/AIDS in parts of sub-Saharan Africa). Iatrogenesis (as with HIV in China and partial tuberculosis treatment in many developing countries), vaccine obstacles and the '10/90 gap' (whereby a minority of health resources are directed towards the most severe health problems) add to this unstable picture.

We inhabit a microbially dominated world. We should therefore frame our relations with microbes primarily in ecological (not military) terms. The world's infectious agents, perhaps with the exceptions of smallpox and polio, will not be eliminated. But much can be done to reduce human population vulnerability and avert conditions conducive to the occurrence of many infectious diseases. This is an important focus for health promotion.

Declining Regional Life Expectancy

The upward trajectory in life expectancy forecast in the 1980s has recently been reversed in several regions, especially in Russia and sub-Saharan Africa. These could, in principle, be either temporary aberrations or unconnected to one another. However, identifiable factors appear to link these declines.

The fall in life expectancy since 1990 in Russia is unprecedented for a technologically developed country. Many proximal causes have been documented, including alcoholism, suicide, violence, accidents and cardiovascular disease. Multiple drug-resistant tuberculosis is widespread in Russian prisons. Collectively, these factors reflect social disintegration and crisis.

In sub-Saharan Africa, HIV/AIDS has combined with poverty, malaria, tuberculosis, depleted soils and undernutrition, deteriorating infrastructure, gender inequality, sexual exploitation and political taboos to foster epidemics that have reduced life expectancy, in some cases drastically. Adverse health and loss of human capital, caused by disease and the out-migration of skilled adults, have helped to 'lock-in' poverty. More broadly, indebtedness and ill-judged economic development policies, including charges for schooling and health services, have also impaired population health in Africa, following decades of earlier improvement. The intersectoral implications for health promotion are clear.

Conflict, most notoriously in Rwanda, has also occurred on a suf-ficient scale to temporarily reduce life expectancy for some populations in sub-Saharan Africa. Age pyramids skewed to young adults have almost certainly played a role in this violence, together with resource scarcity, pre-existing ethnic tensions, poor governance and international inactivity when crises develop.

Global Environmental Change

Sustainable population health depends on the viability of the planet's life-support systems. For humans, achieving and maintaining good population health is the true goal of sustainability, dependent, in turn, on achieving sustainable supportive social, economic and environmental conditions. Today, however, human-induced global environmental changes pose risks to health on unprecedented spatial and temporal scales. These environmental changes, evident at worldwide scale, include climate change, biodiversity loss, downturns in productivity of land and oceans, freshwater depletion and disruption of major elemental cycles (e.g. environmental nitrification). In coming decades, these long-term change processes will exact an increasing health toll via physical hazards, infectious diseases, food and water shortages, conflict and an inter-linked decline in societal capacity.

We currently extract 'goods and services' from the world's natural environment about 25% faster than they can be replenished. Our waste products are also spilling over (e.g. carbon dioxide in the atmosphere). Hence, there is now little unused global 'biocapacity'. We are thus bequeathing an increasingly depleted and disrupted natural world to future generations. Although the resultant adverse health effects are likely to impinge unequally and, often, after time lag, this decline could eventually harm, albeit at varying levels, the entire human population.

Global climate change now attracts particular attention. Fossil fuel combustion, in particular, has caused unprecedented concentrations of atmospheric greenhouse gases. The majority expert view is that human-induced climate change is now underway. The power of storms, long predicted by climate change modellers to increase, appears (in combination with reduced wetlands and failure to maintain infrastructure) to have contributed to the 2005 New Orleans flood. WHO has estimated that, globally, over 150 000 deaths annually result from recent change in the world's climate relative to the baseline average climate of 1961-1990. This number will increase for at least the next several decades.

The most direct risks to future health from climate change are posed by heatwaves, exempli-fied by the estimated 25 000 extra deaths in Europe in August 2003, storms and floods.

Climate-sensitive biotic systems will also be affected. This includes: (i) the vector-pathogen host relationships involved in transmission of various infections, vector-borne and other, (ii) the production of aeroallergens and (iii) the agro-ecosystems that generate food. Recent changes in infectious disease occurrence in some locations-tickborne encephalitis in Sweden, cholera outbreaks in Bangladesh and, possibly, malaria in the east African highlands may partly reflect regional climatic changes.

Changes in the world's climate and ecosystems, biodiversity losses and other large-scale environmental stresses will, in combination, affect the productivity of local agro-ecosystems, freshwater quality and supplies and the habitability, safety and productivity of coastal zones. Such impacts will cause economic dislocation and population displacement. Conflicts and migrant flows are likely to increase, potentiating violence, injury, infectious diseases, malnutrition, mental disorders and other health problems.

These and other categories of global environmental changes, often acting in combination, pose serious health risks to current and future human societies (Figure 1). The important message here is that, increasingly, human health is influenced by socio-economic and environmental changes that originate well beyond national or local boundaries. The major, perhaps irreversible, changes to the biosphere's life-support system, including its climate system, increase the likelihood of adverse intergenerational health impacts.

Emerging health Issues and MDGS

In 2000, UN member states agreed on eight MDGs, with targets to be achieved by 2015. Four MDGs refer explicitly to health outcomes: eradicating extreme poverty and hunger, reducing child mortality, improving maternal health and combating HIV/AIDS, malaria and other infectious diseases.

Many of the MDG targets are already in jeopardy. Although all are inter-linked, the 'environmental sustainability' MDG has fundamental long-term importance. Without it, the other concomitants of sustainability-economic productivity, social stability and, most importantly, population health-are unachievable. An additional reason to advance the MDGs is because that will slow population growth rates and thus reduce our collective ecological footprint.

Faltering Demographic and Epidemiological Transitions

Both the demographic and epidemiological transitions are less orderly than predicted. In some regions, declining fertility rates have overshot the rate needed for an economically and socially optimal age structure. In other countries, population growth has declined substantially because of the reduced life expectancy. Relatedly, the future health dividend from recent reductions in poverty may be lower than that once hoped because of the emergence of the non-communicable 'diseases of affluence', including those due to obesity, dietary imbalances, tobacco use and air pollution.

In the 1960s, there was widespread concern over imminent famine, affecting much of the developing world. This problem was largely averted by the 'Green Revolution' during the 1970s and 1980s. Meanwhile, the earlier view that unconstrained population growth had little adverse impact upon environmental amenity and other conditions needed for human wellbeing gained strength. However, in the last few years, this position has been re-evaluated. There is an increasing recognition of the adverse effects of rapid population growth, especially in developing countries, including from high unemployment when population increase outstrips opportunity.

Some argue that unsustainable regional population growth is characterised by age pyramids excessively skewed to young age, high levels of under- and unemployment and intense competition for limited resources. These circumstances jeopardise public health. Where there is also significant inequality and/or ethnic tension, catastrophic violence can result.

Although Russia and parts of sub-Saharan Africa have vastly different demographic characteristics, there are important similarities in their recent declines in life expectancy. Both regions have a significant scarcity of public goods for health. In Russia, there is a lack of equality, safety and public health services. In many parts of sub-Saharan Africa, there is inadequate governance and food security as well as public safety and public health services. Viewed on an even larger scale, the miserable conditions for millions of people in these regions accord with a global class system, in which privileged groups in both developed and developing countries act to protect their own position at the expense of others.

The growth of the global population and its environmental impact means that we may now be less than a generation from exhausting the biosphere's environmental buffer, unless we can rein in our excessive demands on the natural world. If not, then the demographic and epidemiological transitions, already faltering, will be further affected. Population growth may then slow not only because of the usual development-associated fertility decrease but also because of persistently high death rates elsewhere.

Meanwhile, the growing awareness of these issues, the publicity of the MDGs, the ongoing campaigns against poverty and Third-World debt, calls for public health to address political violence and the renewed vigour of social movements for health affords new potential resources and collaborations to the global health promotion effort. These should be welcomed and acted upon.

Globalisation, Trade, Economic Policy and Faltering Global Public Health

The health benefits of the complex social, cultural, trade and economic phenomena that comprise 'globalisation' are vigorously debated. Although differing viewpoints are inevitable, the strength of this debate signifies that the net gain for population health from globalisation is uncertain. Several important health dividends often attributed to globalisation have plausible alternative explanations. Many health gains in developing countries may be the time-lagged result of development policies and technologies introduced before the era of structural adjustment and partial economic liberalisation, which heralded modern globalisation. The accelerated demographic transition in China is a greatly under-recognised role in that country's rapidly growing wealth, as were China's earlier investments in health and education.

Proponents of gobalisation assert that free trade, via 'comparative advantage', will benefit all populations. In reality, wealthy populations have long tilted the economic and political playing field in ways that ensure a disproportionate flow of trade benefits towards privileged populations. A powerful realpolitic impediment to the complete removal of trade-distorting national subsidies is that this would probably entail a relatively greater loss for wealthy populations than for the poor. In contrast, the economic disadvantages incurred to date through partial market deregulation have largely been confined to relatively poor and politically weak populations in developed countries.

The pre-eminence of modern economic theory presents a major obstacle for health promoters. The narrow focus of the World Trade Organisation, which largely discounts the often adverse social, environmental and public health impacts of trade, underscores the problem. Dominant economic theory evolved when environmental limits were considered remote. These theories assume that increased per capita income will offset the noncosted losses, whether these affect social welfare, environmental resources or public health. Critiques of these theories note that the harshest costs of modern economic practices fall upon ecosystems and populations with little current economic power or value, including generations not yet born.

Mobility of capital brings development, but capricious capital flight can create great hardship, including for public health. Deregulated labour conditions facilitate cheap goods, but they concentrate occupational health hazards among powerless workers. Increased labour mobility and steep economic gradients weaken family and community structures, contribute to 'brain drain' and promote inter-ethnic tensions.

Many indices of inequality, including in health, income and environmental risk, have risen in recent decades. Most critical commentary of globalisation is conceptual, emphasizing the adverse experiences of the disadvantaged and unborn. In contrast, the experiential feedback of the main beneficiaries of modern economic policy is largely positive. A major challenge for the promoters of health (and other forms) of justice is to adduce stronger evidence to convince policy-makers (themselves largely benefi-ciaries of globalisation) to promote public goods, even though this may diminish the relative privilege of policy-makers and their constituencies. This is a difficult but essential task for health promotion.

Emerging Health Issues

In sum, global and regional inequality, narrow and outdated economic theories and an evernearing set of global environmental limits endanger population health. On the positive side of the ledger, there have been some gains (e.g. literacy, information sharing and food production, and new medical and public health technologies continue to confer large health benefits). Overall, though, reliance on economic, especially market-based, processes to achieve social goals and to set priorities and on technological fixes for environmental problems is poorly attuned to the long-term improvement of global human well-being and health. For that, a transformation of social institutions and norms and, hence, of public policy priorities is needed. Population health can be a powerful lever in that process of social change, if health promotion can rise to this challenge.

Many of these contemporary risks to population health affect entire systems and social-cultural processes, in contrast to the continuing health risks from personal/ family behaviours and localised environmental exposures. These newly recognised risks to health derive from demographic shifts, large-scale environmental changes, an economic system that emphasizes the material over other elements of well being and the cultural and behavioural changes accompanying development. Together, these emerging health risks present a huge challenge to which the wider community is not yet attuned. The risks fall outside the popular conceptual frame wherein health is viewed in relation to personal behaviours, local environmental pollutants, doctors and hospitals. In countries that promote individual choice and responsibility, there are few economic incentives for the population's health.

Health promotion must, of course, continue to deal with the many local and immediate health problems faced by individuals, families and communities. But to do so without also seeking to guide socio-economic development and the forms and policies of regional and international governance is to risk being 'penny wise but pound foolish'. Tackling these more systemic health issues requires multi-sectoral policy coordination at community, national and international levels, via an expanded repertoire of bottom-up, top-down and 'middle-out' approaches to health promotion.

Gender and Health Promotion

In most countries, resources allocated by government to health-promoting activities are very limited compared to investments in medical care. This imbalance is evident also in the richest countries of the world. For example, in the USA, approximately 95% of the health expenditure goes to direct medical care services, whereas only 5% is allocated to prevention activities. In Canada, the medical care systems absorbs the majority of health sector resources, with less than 3% of health spending allocated towards health promotion. Therefore, it is of utmost importance to invest these limited resources in preventive activities with high potential for success and cost-effectiveness. In the first section of this paper, we argue that health promotion policies that take women's and men's differential biological and social vulnerability to health risks into account are more likely to be successful and cost-effective compared to policies that are not concerned with such differences.

There is overwhelming evidence from all fields of health research that women and men are different as regards their biology (sex differences), their access to and control over resources and their decision-making power in the family and community, as well as the roles and responsibilities that society assigns to them (gender differences). Together gender and sex, often in interaction with socioeconomic circumstances, influence exposure to health risks, access to health information and services, health outcomes and the social and economic consequences of ill-health. Recognising the root causes of gender inequities in health is crucial therefore when designing health system responses. Health promotion as well as disease prevention needs to address these differences between women and men, boys and girls in an equitable manner in order to be effective.

Today, there is a growing recognition, among health professionals, researchers and policymakers, of the widespread and profound implications of gender-based inequities in health. There is also emerging evidence that integrating gender considerations into interventions has a positive effect on health outcomes across various domains. Even though knowledge of gender differences in health is increasingly available, it does not always translate easily into realities of health planning and programme implementation.

The field of health promotion is no exception: the lack of translation of knowledge about gender inequities in health into health promotion interventions leads to misallocated resources and weakened potential for success. For example, violence against women, arguably the most extreme phenomenon of gender inequality, affects millions of women. Until recently, the magnitude and health consequences of domestic violence against women have been neglected in both research and policy.

We have now clear evidence that gender-based violence causes physical and psychological harm. In addition, it undermines the social, economic, spiritual and emotional well-being of the survivor, the perpetrator and society as a whole, but it also compromises the trust relationship between men and women. The social, economic, psychological, physical, emotional and relationship harm to individuals from gender-based violence constitutes a major health concern that requires creative and imaginative responses from the plethora of policymakers and intervention agencies dealing with health promotion and prevention of violence. In particular, lack of attention to the hidden emotional outcome of gender-based violence, loss of trust, loss of dignity and a deeply compromised self-esteem need to be addressed alongside housing, economic support, social welfare and legal issues as part of an integrated health promotion strategy.

Gender blindness

When planning and implementing health promotion and disease prevention strategies, gender is an issue that is often neglected. Generally, there seems to be an assumption that interventions will be just as effective for men as for women. Many health promotion programmes are gender blind and based on research where the sex of the study participants is not made explicit. Gender-neutral expressions, such as 'health care providers', 'children', 'adolescents' or 'employees', are often used in programme descriptions and reports. As a result, collection, analysis and presentation of data are often not sex-disaggregated and no gender analysis is undertaken.

Terminology is crucial in framing gendered responses to health promotion challenges. For example, the WHO Multi-country Study authors recommend using the term 'genderbased violence' to replace the commonly used descriptive terms: intimate partner violence (denotes relationship to perpetrator), domestic violence (denotes location of the abuse) and violence against women (denotes the sex of the survivor). This ensures that the cause of the violence is not forgotten. Violence is regularly the product of socialised but mutable gender relationships, and this is written into the term 'gender-based violence'. Relationship problems take centre stage with risky behaviour, social disadvantage, environmental degradation and germs in the aetiological chain of events that lead to ill-health and compromised well-being. Health promotion initiatives need to recognise the importance of good gender relationships in promoting health and well-being.

Gender' as a proxy for 'women'

Health promotion involves the agent of promotion and the beneficiary of it. In this context, the social construction of gender roles come into play as many of the promotional measures are put into action by women being the care guarantor of every individual in the household. Consequently, health promotion messages often target women in their assigned role as caregivers in the family. Since women's ability to make decisions about implementing health promotional measures is often limited in many countries due to their lower status in the household, the positive health effects of the promotional measures may be less than expected. When health promotion campaigns are addressed to the family as a whole and to the relationships between males and females of all ages, health programmes can be considerably improved.

In Ghana, information about the importance of child immunisation was directed to both fathers and mothers. As a result, men have taken greater responsibility for their children's health, leading to increased vaccination rates and earlier immunisation. In Lao PDR, an outreach health promotion programme attached to the Bolikhan District Maternity Waiting Home targeted men in 11 remote Hmong and Lao villages to encourage them to take an active role in reproductive health. Interactive sessions addressed male and female anatomy and function, fertilisation, physiology of pregnancy, birth spacing including responsibility of men, sexually transmittal infections and HIV prevention, the importance of antenatal and postnatal care, nutrition and relaxation during pregnancy. Attendance rates were over 80% of the men in each village. Before the programme, only 18% of participants said they had a very good knowledge of reproductive health issues. At the end of the programme, 72% of participants reported very good knowledge. Thus gendered knowledge barriers to health improvement were greatly reduced in all 11 villages.

Focus on behavioural change

Many health promotion strategies aim at reducing risky behaviours, such as smoking, while ignoring the material, social and psychological conditions within which the targeted behaviours are embedded. For example, in many countries there is a strong association between material hardship, low social status, stressful work or life events and smoking prevalence. Critics have argued that gender roles and health-related behaviours linked to those roles in many health promotion programmes have led to a focus on behavioural change at the individual level, rather than on policy change at the societal level.

Prevention strategies to reduce harmful stress among working women often include measures where the onus is put on women to develop their own personal stress coping strategies to balance competing gender roles. Targeted women often feel accused of not being able to cope with multiple pressures arising from their responsibilities as mothers, wives, housekeepers and workers. To avoid this, complementary measures to ease women's burden, such as the universal provision of accessible and affordable day-care centres for children and the introduction of more flexible working hours, should also be introduced.

Similarly, many men may experience extraordinary pressures from unemployment and material hardship, which constrain them to fulfil their assigned gender role as 'breadwinners'. Those who try to cope with stresses through behaviours, such as smoking, drinking or drug abuse, are accused of risking their health by their own personal choice. Strategies that aim at changing the lifestyles of these men would probably be more effective if combined with measures to change the social environment in which the health damaging lifestyles are embedded.

According to a study from Thailand, although the nationwide '100% condom programme' to prevent HIV infection has led to a decrease of the infection among men, young women who were engaged in commercial sex have not been protected from the infection to the same degree as men. Obviously, there is a need for policies that recognise and address the gender differences of status and power that structure sexual relationships and counteract women's lack of assertiveness to insist on condom use. Again the issue of trust in the relationships between men and women is a key factor for health promotion programmes to take into account.

Lack of multisectoral approach

Traditionally, the health field has been predominantly the domain of medical professionals and the health care sector, where the main focus is on individual health and individual risk factors. Therefore, health promotion and disease prevention strategies within the health care sector are often limited to individual health advice, e.g. on smoking cessation.

One limitation of this is that certain groups of people, such as the poor who cannot afford user fees or women who cannot without permission from their husbands visit health clinics, will be excluded from health advice and information. Another limitation is that the promotional measures within the health care sector are unable to tackle the root causes of health disparities. Many of the health determinants need to be tackled by policies in sectors where health is created, such as the labour market, social services, education system, housing, environmental protection, water and sanitation, transport, road safety and security. These policies have direct and indirect health impacts, which may differ between men and women.

The understanding that both women's and men's health is dependent on several societal sectors is critical to upstream, multisectoral health promoting policies and interventions. Any such initiative should take into account the involvement of key stakeholders in communities and needs to be acceptable at individual, household as well as societal levels. In many traditional communities, traditional chiefs, or village leaders, act as gatekeepers in all educational and community-based activities, so it is essential to incorporate these key stakeholders in any health promotion policies and interventions designed to reduce gender inequities.

Top-down approach

The traditional public health approach is top-down rather than bottom-up, with experts identifying problems and formulating interventions while the problems and solutions as perceived by those at particular risk rarely constitute the base for action. The power of change is then defined primarily in political and professional terms without the possibility of the targeted people to influence and control various determinants of health. Because of power imbalances and because of the low representation of women in decisionmaking bodies, women can seldom make their voices heard.

As a result, health promotion programmes designed in a top-down manner will not necessarily correspond to women's health needs. Health promotion policies and activities are most meaningful when target communities and groups are involved in all aspects of policy and programme development, implementation and evaluation. For example, 'The Blue Nile Health Project' in Sudan with the objective to control water associated diseases was perceived as very successful, thanks to the particular emphasis in the programme on gender-related aspects that defined women's role and participation.

Joint commitment

Through international agreements, such as the Ottawa Charter for Health Promotion and the WHO Health For All Strategy, many countries have already committed themselves to health promotion. Likewise, most countries in the world have committed themselves to promote gender equity. These agreements state that all women and men have the right to live without discrimination in all spheres of life, including access to health care, education and equal remuneration for equal work. The recently adopted Bangkok Charter for Health Promotion states that health promotion contributes, among other things, to reducing both health and gender inequities.

Some major achievements in working towards gender equity are evident. For example, the Multi-country Study on Health and Domestic Violence against Women acknowledges the 'combined efforts of grass-roots and international women's organisations, international experts and committed governments' in producing 'a profound transformation of public awareness' about gender-based violence. Since the World Conference on Human Rights, the International Conference on Population and Development and the Fourth World Conference on Women, the perception of gender-based violence as purely a welfare and justice issue has changed significantly to the point where violence against women is 'now widely recognised as a serious human rights abuse' as well as 'an important public health problem that concerns all sectors'. However, as the 10-year reviews of the ICPD Plan of Action and the Beijing Platform for Action have highlighted, all countries still have a long way to go to achieve gender equity in all areas of health and well-being.

The internationally agreed Millennium Development Goals (MDGs) identified 'gender equality and empowerment of women' as the third of eight goals and a condition for achieving the other seven. Although, these and similar commitmentshave been ratified by most United Nations Member States, action by governments to bring national laws, policies and practices in line with the provisions of the rati-fied conventions has lagged behind. Moreover, these commitments have not been pursued in the health sector. The Beijing Declaration and Platform for Action in 1995 as well as the UN Economic and Social Council in 1997 have clearly established 'gender mainstreaming' as the global strategy for promoting, among other things, women's health. In the field of public health, this strategy means the integration of both women's and men's concerns into the formulation, monitoring and analysis of policies, programmes and projects. In relation to health promotion, it entails taking into account gender issues that have implications for individual and community health.

Setting international, national and local objectives for gender equity in health is the first step in establishing a joint commitment. These objectives need to be measurable and translated into policies and actions. A good example of translating international objectives to promote gender equity and health into national objectives comes from Lao PDR. The Lao Ministries of Health and Education have signed, in response to the need to meet the targets of the MDGs, a memorandum of understanding to collaborate in developing health promotion programmes in Lao primary schools, which address all eight targets including MDG 3 to promote gender equity. In combination with the Lao Women's Union, village health committees, NGOs and international organisations, the Lao government ministries have also developed a multisectoral national development plan to mainstream gender into all areas of health and well-being.

Assessment and analysis of gender inequities in health

In order to maximise efficient use of resources, health promoting strategies and actions, in general, need to be based on an assessment of the size, nature and root causes of gender inequalities in health. More specifically, health promotion relating to certain issues, for example, gender-based violence, HIV/AIDS, malaria, nutrition or smoking, needs to be designed with an understanding of how women and men differ in relation to the issue's causes, manifestations and consequences. Collection, analysis and reporting of data disaggregated by sex, age, socioeconomic status, education, ethnicity and geographic location should be performed systematically by individual research projects or through larger data systems. Attention needs to be paid to the possibility that data may reflect systematic gender biases due to inadequate methodologies that fail to capture women's and men's different realities. The promotion of gendersensitive research to inform the development, implementation, monitoring and evaluation of health promotion policies and programs is also desirable.

One good example of recording sexdisaggregated, gender-sensitive and genderspecific health data comes from Malaysia. In 2000, the Asian-Pacific Resource and Research Centre for Women (ARROW) published 'A

Framework of Indicators for Action on Women's Health Needs & Rights after Beijing'. This publication was developed as a tool for all government, non-government and international organisations to use in monitoring implementation of the Beijing Platform for Action.

The framework presents selected Beijing recommendations on women's health and rights, sexual and reproductive health, violence against women and gender-sensitive health programmes, which are then operationalised into quantitative and qualitative indicators. These can be measured to assess progress particularly in women's health status; health service provision, use and quality; and national laws, policies and plans. This will be reviewed in a publication to be released in late 2006. Meanwhile, Arrow has applied a similar framework in its 'Monitoring Ten Years of ICPD Implementation'.

Eight countries in the Asia Pacific region were examined in detail, using indicators derived from the ICPD recommendations, to 'assess progress in policies, laws and services and changes in women's health, status and lives' over the past 10 years and to 'identify the main barriers and facilitating factors in implementing commitments made in the Programme of Action, ICPD'. The Report reveals that 10 years after ICPD, 'women's lives have seen only minimal improvement' and 'violence against women is on the rise, as is HIV/ AIDS transmission for women and men' . The Report argues that 'one of the best indicators of real change in power relations between men and women is a decrease in domestic violence and rape' yet 'only two of the eight countries had ever had a national prevalence survey on domestic violence' let alone put prevention strategies in place.

The health promotion recommendations that emerge form the 2005 ARROW Report suggest a major rethinking of intervention to deal with key challenges. These challenges include: deeply embedded patriarchy, early marriage and early first parity, declining commitment of service providers, lack of political will and stability, social inequities, religious fundamentalism in some areas, trends to privatisation, liberalisation and globalisation and persistent low levels of literacy among women and girls.

Key recommendations for health promotion include niche planning by governments, rather than the use of uniform 'one size fits all' health promotion programmes, using NGOs as clearing houses for up-to-date dissemination of data and community-based workshops on a variety of health issues and using traditional authority processes to run campaigns to promote female literacy and education.

Gender analysis of sex-disaggregated data revealed important differences between adolescent boys and girls concerning patterns of physical activity. First, girls were more involved in vigorous physical activity than boys, which was a surprise because literature from several developed countries suggested the opposite. Further analysis showed that the main reason behind this was girls' involvement in strenuous housekeeping (42% of girls versus 6% of boys). On the other hand, boys utilised more active transportation to and from school (100% of boys versus 57% of girls). This was a very important source of information for the programme managers for the design of intervention to increase physical activity among girls and boys.

Social and environmental determinants of gender inequities in health

The prime determinants of gender inequities in health are social and economic disadvantages related to factors such as decision-making power, income, employment, working environment, education, housing, nutrition and individual behaviours.

Women and men are exposed to various risk factors to different degrees due to differences in gender roles and living and working conditions. These differences are crucial to recognise, estimate and monitor when designing interventions, programmes and population-wide risk reduction strategies. Many determinants of gender inequities in health can be influenced by healthpromoting measures and risk reduction strategies ranging from micro- to macro-public policy levels. Keleher emphasizes the need for sustainable upstream strategies that address the economic, social and cultural obstacles that prevent women from fulfilling their potential. She argues that such strategies are much more likely to bring about sustainable change than a continual reliance on midstream and downstream strategies.

Actions to strengthen individuals Many health promoting interventions with a gender perspective have focussed mainly on strengthening women's and girls' capacity to better respond to, and control determinants of, health in the physical and social environment. They include gaining access to economic capital as well as social and cultural capital. The most effective interventions are those with an empowerment focus. They aim to help women to: gain knowledge about, and access to, their rights; access microcredit to start their own businesses; improve their access to essential services; address perceived deficiencies in their knowledge (including literacy and secondary education); acquire personal skills and thereby improve their health. Empowerment initiatives aim to encourage both sexes to challenge gender stereotypes. Such actions can include, for example, training boys and men to reduce gender biases by promoting gender-sensitive behaviour and reducing violence. Another example of such initiatives is raising awareness among young girls and their families about unfair discrimination against girls and thereby promoting the status and a value of the girl child. The Girl Child Project in Pakistan has, for example, made girls aware that unequal food allocation in the family is wrong.

Actions to strengthen communities Strengthening communities can cover a wide spectrum of strategies aimed at strengthening the way deprived communities function collectively for mutual support and benefit. These range from helping to create meeting places and facilities for social interaction to supporting communities' defence against health hazards, such as substance abuse, crime and violence or environmental pollution. For example, several innovative and gender-sensitive community level initiatives have emerged in Africa over the past decade in response to the devastating effects of the AIDS epidemic in the region.

One of these initiatives is the Community Life Project in Lagos, Nigeria, which is a unique example of how synergistic partnerships between activists, community and religious organisations, local institutions, involving men, women and children simultaneously, can help to effectively break the silence on sexuality issues. The project is working with 23 community groups to increase and sustain HIV/AIDS awareness in the community; addressing HIV/ AIDS within the broader framework of sexual and reproductive health through sexuality education sessions; and increasing community ownership and participation by training representatives of the groups as volunteers and family life educators. Thus, the initiative places sexuality education on the community's agenda, thereby creating a supportive environment for advancing women's reproductive and sexual health.

In the Woorabinda Aboriginal community in rural Queensland, Australia, the community has organised sanctions around the weekend Australian Rules Football match related to gender-based violence. Any player who has been identified as having abused his partner during any week is banned by the team committee from playing in the football match at the weekend. This reinforces community and shared abhorrence of gender-based violence and acts as a public endorsement of good relations between men and women in the community.

Actions to promote gender equity in access to essential facilities and services In both industrialised and developing countries, improvements in living and working conditions and access to services have been shown to bring substantial health improvements to populations. Public health initiatives influencing living and working conditions include measures to improve access to clean water, adequate nutrition and housing, sanitation, safer workplaces and health and other welfare services. Policies within these areas are normally the responsibility of separate sectors and there is a need for them to cooperate in order to improve the health of the population.

Health promotion policies and interventions aimed at improving living and working conditions and access to services need to be particularly gender sensitive due to the fact that women and men face distinct health risks in their living and working environment and have different health needs. For example, many developing countries suffer from weak health services, infrastructures and unaffordable services, a situation that disproportionately affects women as they require more preventive reproductive health services. The inadequacy and lack of affordability of health services is compounded by physical and cultural barriers to care. At the national level, some attempts have been made to tackle cost and affordability barriers in health services to women. For example, South Africa and Sri Lanka provide free maternal and infant health services. In some cultures, women are reluctant to consult male doctors. The lack of female medical personnel is an important barrier to utilisation of health services for many women.

To overcome this barrier, the Women's Health Project in Pakistan works with the Ministry of Health to improve the health of women, girls and infants in 20 predominantly rural districts in four provinces through measures, such as the expansion of communitybased health care and family planning services through the recruitment and training of thousands of village women as Lady Health Workers, a 'safe delivery' campaign, and the promotion of women's health and nutritional needs and family planning. The project assumes that a female health care provider could better understand the problem of another woman.

Actions to encourage social and economic policy change Policies at the structural level include economic and social policies spanning sectors such as labour market, trade environment and more general efforts to improve women's status. These policies have a great potential to reduce or exacerbate gender inequality, including inequities in health. Influencing factors affecting social stratification is therefore a key for the improvement of women's social position relative to men. Policies aimed at improving women's education, increasing their possibilities to earn an income within the labour market, giving women access to micro-credit to start small businesses and family welfare policies are all measures for improving women's social status in the family and in the society. Improved social status for women relative to men may improve women's control over household resources and their own lives. For example, development policies in Matlab (Bangladesh) included strategies, such as micro-credit schemes linked to employment and provision of more places in school for daughters of poor families, which successfully increased the status of the poorest women.

Equity-oriented policies in a social context in which women had traditional matrilineal rights to property and girls were valued as much as boys have resulted in considerable health gains in Kerala, India. Women could benefit from improvements in health care provision and achieve high levels of literacy. Kerala is the only state in India where the population sex ratio has been favourable to women throughout the 20th century, and it is not plagued by the problem of 'missing women'. Increasing the participation of women in political and other decisionmaking processes-at household, community and national levels-and ensuring that laws and their implementation do not discriminate against women are measures that have a great potential to improve gender equality and health equity.

The examples presented earlier suggest that most successful interventions are those that combine a wide range of intersectoral and upstream approaches as well as downstream interventions to tackle a problem. For example, interventions at the individual level to empower women to deal with the threats to their mental and physical health from violence are important. However, interventions are also needed at the structural level, where governments have a central role in policy and legislation and in mandating organisational change to ensure that women are in the position to be empowered. The establishment of societal freedoms from discrimination and violence must sit alongside other efforts to increase women's access to economic resources and social inclusion. These economic, legal, social and cultural assets are fundamental to generating and maintaining women's health and well-being but they also benefit men.

Documenting and disseminating effective and gender-sensitive policy interventions to promote health There is a paucity of information on costeffective and gender-sensitive health promoting strategies and interventions that have successfully addressed social determinants of health, and little concrete guidance is available to policymakers. Developing an international reporting system to collect such information in order to increase the accessibility for policymakers to relevant information needs to be encouraged. Monitoring and evaluation of strategies and interventions are also important for informing future processes and track progress towards gender equality.

Indicators and methods should be developed urgently for systematic integration of gender dimensions in health impact assessments that assess not only a policy's impact at an aggregate level, but on different population groups, including the marginalised and vulnerable; such an assessment should be applicable not only to health systems policy, but also to policy in other sectors.

Promoting Mental Health

It is of great concern that mental health promotion is frequently overlooked as an integral part of health promotion. This is surprising because, in theory, mental health is accepted as an essential component of health, the close relationship between physical and mental health is recognised and it is generally known that physical and mental health share many of the same social, environmental and economic determinants. We know that facilities for those with mental health problems are more poorly resourced than those for physical illness in many parts of the world and it is important that mental health promotion does not get similarly affected.

Relationship between Health Promotion and Mental Health Promotion

Health is defined by the World Health Organisation (WHO) as 'a state of complete physical, mental and social well-being and not merely the absence of disease or infirmity' and health promotion is understood as 'actions that support people to adopt and maintain healthy lifestyles and which create supportive living conditions or environments for health'.

In these definitions it is clearly recognised that mental health promotion is an integral component of health promotion. Not only are there complex interconnections between physical and mental health, they share many of the same determinants. Therefore, while mental health promotion will focus more specifically on the determinants of mental health and the creation of conditions that enable optimum psychological and psychophysiological development, these efforts will impact positively on physical health.

Two of the five strategies set out in the Ottawa Charter for Health Promotion 'strengthen community action' and 'develop personal skills'-essentially refer to mental health promotion activities: for example, programmes aimed at reducing social inequality and building social capital. It is also recognised that strategies that maximise the active ownership and participation of people in health promotion initiatives contribute positively to the sustainability of the programmes. In this sense health promotion is facilitated by mental health promotion. Conversely, when the focus of the intervention is more directly on the promotion of mental health, physical health issues must not be ignored.

Mental health can be understood as:

> a state of well-being in which the individual realises his or her own abilities, can cope with the normal stresses of life, can work productively and fruitfully, and is able to make a contribution to his or her own community.

Other definitions of mental health refer to the individual's subjective feelings of well-being, optimism and mastery, the concepts of 'resilience', or the ability to deal with adversity, and the capacity to be able to form and maintain meaningful relationships. Although the expression of these qualities will differ contextually and individually from culture to culture, the basic qualities remain the same.

Relationship between Physical and Mental Health

The artificial division of 'physical health' from 'mental health' common in the western developed world is not shared by many traditional cultures in which physical conditions have long been considered as being closely related to the emotional, social or spiritual health of the person.

The reciprocal relationship between physical and mental health now is widely recognised. It is known that mental well-being, social support and social networks are protective factors for physical health. Positive mental health significantly assists people to deal with physical conditions. Conversely, the promotion of physical health impacts positively on mental health, for example, in older people. It is recognised that diabetes, cancer, cardiovascular disease and HIV/AIDS affect and are affected by the mental state of individuals, and particularly by depression. Heart disease is found to double in people with depression and approximately one-half of people with heart disease suffer an episode of major depression.

Clearly, to be effective, promotion and prevention programmes addressing health conditions should take mental health factors into account, and mental health and health programmes are best implemented together.

Burden of Mental Ill-Health

Apart from aiming to increase positive mental health, mental health promotion has an important role to play in relation to mental disorders, in that positive mental health is a strong protective factor against mental disorders. Mental health promotion includes 'strategies to promote the mental well-being of those who are not at risk, those who are at increased risk and those who are suffering or recovering from mental health problems'.

The size and cost of the burden of mental and behavioural disorders is perhaps not fully appreciated. Mental and behavioural disorders represented 11% of the total disease burden in 1990, and this is expected to rise to 15% by 2020. Five of the 10 leading causes of disability worldwide in 1990 were mental or behavioural disorders. Depression was the fourth largest contributor to the disease burden in 1990 and is expected to rank second after ischaemic heart disease by 2020. It is estimated that one in four people will develop one or more mental or behavioural disorders in their life-time and that one in four families has one member suffering from a mental or behavioural disorder.

The social and economic costs of only attempting to deal with these issues through individual and treatment paradigms is not only prohibitive, but impossible in many parts of the world where there are few mental health professionals. A public health approach to mental health promotion is imperative, in which, in addition to treatment, efforts are made to support the factors that have been shown to promote mental health and address the factors that constitute risk factors for mental disorders. Unless this is done, the burden of mental illness will continue to grow.

Global Health Promotion

As globalisation increasingly impacts on diverse aspects of our lives, we are beginning to understand how factors that go beyond the national borders of individual countries are influencing the determinants of health and health outcomes. This chapter discusses what is meant by 'global health promotion' in terms of the process of enabling people to increase control over, and to improve, their health within an increasingly global context. The focus of this paper is the extent to which global governance architecture is emerging for health promotion. After briefly reviewing the concepts of global health governance (GHG), this paper draws lessons from selected examples of global health promotion initiatives and concludes with suggested strategies for building a global approach to health promotion.

From International to Global Governance

Governance concerns the many ways in which people organise themselves to achieve common goals. Such collective action requires agreed rules, norms and institutions on such matters as membership within the cooperative relationship, distribution of authority, decision-making processes, means of communication and resource mobilisation and allocation. Health governance concerns the agreed rules, norms and institutions that collectively promote and protect health.

Importantly, while government can be a central component of governance, governance more broadly embraces the contributions of other social actors, notably civil society organisations (CSOs) and the corporate sector. Moreover, governance embraces a variety of mechanisms, both formal (e.g. law, treaty and code of practice) and informal (e.g. norms and custom). Formal instruments with the strongest regulatory powers can be legally binding and backed by punitive measures (e.g. fines or imprisonment). Informal mechanisms may rely on self-regulation and voluntary compliance, as well as less tangible forms of censure, such as public opinion.

Global health governance GHG can be distinguished from international health governance (IHG) in three ways. First, IHG involves crossborder cooperation between governments concerned foremost with the health of their domestic populations. Infectious disease surveillance, monitoring and reporting, regulation of trade in health services and protection of patented drugs under the Agreement on Trade-Related Intellectual Property Rights (TRIPS) are examples of IHG. However, changes being brought about by globalisation mean that many health determinants and outcomes are becoming increasingly difficult to confine within a given territorial boundary (i.e. country) and, in some cases, are becoming de-linked from physical space (deterritorialised). As such, it has been argued that the current IHG architecture alone is inadequate to deal with transborder flows that impact on health, such as people trafficking, global climate change and internet pharmaceutical sales.

Second, the mechanisms of IHG are, by defi-nition, focused on governments in terms of authority and enforcement. Examples include the International Health Regulations (IHR) and Framework Convention on Tobacco Control (FCTC). In contrast, GHG embraces both governmental and non-governmental actors and a wider range of formal and informal governance mechanisms. These include voluntary codes of practice, quality control standards, accreditation methods and consumer monitoring and reporting. These mechanisms vary widely in their jurisdiction, purpose, scope and associated resources.

Third, while IHG is traditionally focused on the health sector, GHG seeks to address the broad determinants of health, extending its reach to health impacts from non-health sectors, such as trade and finance, and environment across multiple levels of governance. As Collin et al. write,

> In a world where many health risks and opportunities are becoming increasingly globalised, influencing health determinants, status and outcomes cannot be achieved through actions taken at the national level alone. The intensification of transborder flows of people, ideas, goods and services necessitates a reassessment of the rules and institutions that govern health policy and practice.

The three distinct features of GHG described above can be understood through the example of efforts to control dengue fever across multiple countries. An IHG approach would concentrate on a coordinated effort by ministries of health in affected countries to tackle environmental factors, distribute bed nets and increase the use of insect repellents. Reporting of data on incidence might be shared among the appropriate public health authorities. In contrast, a GHG approach would consider the role of transborder factors, such as documented and undocumented migration, and migration of the Aedes aegypti mosquito.

In addition to government, there might be cooperation among a wide range of relevant stakeholders such as non-governmental organisations (NGOs), private companies, research institutions and local communities. Finally, the impacts on the social and natural environment from changes to agricultural practices (e.g. agribusiness), terms of trade, or conflict and political instability would be taken into account. To the extent that globalisation requires global governance architecture for health, there is a need to rethink traditional approaches to health promotion. There is a need to understand how globalisation, defined as changes that are intensifying crossborder and transborder flows of people and other life forms, trade and finance and knowledge and ideas, is impacting on the process of enabling people to increase control over, and to improve, their health. For example:

— The promotion of sexual health may require greater attention to changing patterns of population mobility within and across countries in the form of migration, tourism, displaced populations and migrant workers.

— The promotion of healthy diets may require measures to counter the marketing of global brands by transnational corporations.

— The promotion of tobacco control may require measures to tackle the availability of contraband cigarettes, and the targeting of emerging markets in low-and middle-income countries by transnational tobacco companies (TTCs).

— The promotion of healthy living environments may require greater attention to the impact of large-scale agricultural production on urbanisation and land availability.

Global health promotion can be defined as the process of enabling people to increase control over, and to improve, their health within an increasingly global context. The challenge lies in creating effective forms of governance that support such efforts. In principle, there is an emergent architecture for global health promotion, as shown in the examples below. By definition, health promotion is broadly conceived to involve a range of social institutions, from governmental bodies to individual families. In practice, however, initiatives to date that seek to tackle global health issues have reflected the uneven quality of existing institutions and shortfalls in how they operate together.

2

Nutritional Interventions through Schools

Healthy nutrition takes many forms and is understood differently in different countries and among different cultures. In general, healthy nutrition should be an integral part of daily life that contributes to the physiological, mental and social well-being of individuals. It is the combined effect of food, health and care. Nutritional well-being is determined by consuming safe food as part of an appropriate and balanced diet that contains adequate amounts of nutrients in relation to bodily requirements. The health and lifestyle of an individual influences the extent to which food contributes to good social, mental and physical well-being. Care is shown by providing time, attention and support in the household and the community to meet the food and health needs of the child and other family members. Furthermore, social ties are validated and maintained by the exchange of food since offering food is associated with offering love, affection and friendship.

Malnutrition

Malnutrition is any physical condition resulting either from an inappropriate or inadequate diet, such as a diet that either provides too much or too little of necessary nutrients, or from a physical inability to absorb or metabolise nutrients. Malnutrition can be related to various factors, such as infections which lead to poor appetite and malabsorption, poverty, and lack of access to food, sanitation and/or health services. Malnutrition negatively affects the quality of life and learning as well as death and disease status.

NUTRITION INTERVENTIONS

Nutrition interventions are policies, services, learning experiences and other actions implemented by schools, individuals or groups to make healthy nutrition a way of daily life. Nutrition interventions are designed to promote health and decrease the risk of disease. In a Health-Promoting School, nutrition interventions are integrated into all aspects of the school and community life, such as the physical and psychosocial environment; a wide variety of educational opportunities; school/community projects; school health services; health promotion for school staff; counselling and social support programmes; physical exercise, recreation and sport; and food programmes.

Efforts to Improve Nutrition

Nutrition is vital to all human beings and to the societies that they comprise. Adequately nourished people enjoy optimal growth, health and well-being. Girls in particular benefit from good nutrition as their health status and eating habits have a major impact on pregnancy, lactation and nourishment of their children.

While over 800 million people are estimated to lack access to food to meet their daily basic needs for energy and protein, more than 3 billion people are deficient in essential micronutrients such as iodine, vitamin A and iron. Many forms of malnutrition exceed the worldwide incidence of most other diseases. For instance, more than half of the 12.2 million deaths every year of children under the age of 5 in developing countries are associated with malnutrition. Thus, efforts are needed to make healthy nutrition accessible for everyone, everywhere and at all times.

Efforts through schools

Schools provide the most effective and efficient way to reach large portions of the population, including young people, school personnel, families and community members. Students can be reached at influential stages in their lives, during childhood and adolescence when lifelong nutritional patterns are formed. Children at every successive year from the earliest grade through secondary school can be addressed. Schools have been given the mandate and responsibility to enhance all aspects of development and maturation of children and youth under qualified guidance.

Furthermore, schools also provide a setting to introduce nutrition information and technologies to the community and can lead the community in advocating policies and services that promote good nutrition. No other setting than schools offers these opportunities on as equal a basis.

Good nutrition strengthens the learning potential and wellbeing of children

Good health and nutrition are needed to achieve one's full educational potential because nutrition affects intellectual development and learning ability. Multiple studies report significant findings between the nutritional status and cognitive test scores or school performance. Consistently, children with more adequate diets score higher on tests of factual knowledge than those with less adequate nutrition. For instance, studies in Honduras,

Kenya and the Philippines show that the academic performance and mental ability of pupils with good nutritional status are significantly higher than those of pupils with poor nutritional status, independent of family income, school quality and teacher ability.

Good nutrition in early life enables healthy adulthood and ageing

Among well nourished people, acute disease and illness tend to be less frequent, less severe and of shorter duration thus providing increased capacities to perform daily activities. Good nutrition also fosters mental, social and physical well-being throughout life; for instance, by strengthening a positive body image and increasing the sense of personal worth. Healthy nutrition can also contribute to a more comfortable life by helping young people to develop healthy teeth and gums. Thus, good nutrition during childhood helps to lay the foundation for a healthy adulthood.

A healthy diet can also contribute to more mobility in older age. For instance, it is likely that youth is a unique time to acquire the strongest possible bones to decrease the risk of osteoporosis in old age. Diets rich in calcium can help build stronger bones while diets rich in protein and salt increase the chances of losing bone density later in life. Thus, it is important to enable children to establish or reinforce personal skills, healthy perceptions and useful knowledge in nutrition to promote their own health and the health of those they care for. It is beneficial to teach persons healthy eating patterns when they are young since eating patterns are established early in life and are difficult to change once they are developed during youth.

Girls will particularly benefit from nutrition interventions

Many of the problems of childbirth, such as haemorrhage, infection and obstructed labour, can be reduced in severity by adequate nutrition earlier in life. For instance, small stature, which may be related to undernutrition, is a well-known risk factor for obstructed labour. Anaemia, which can result from inadequate intake of iron-rich foods, lack of iron supplements or parasite infection, is known to cause about one-fifth of maternal deaths during pregnancy and childbirth.

Women's social roles can also be enhanced through nutrition interventions in areas where women primarily perform the role of preparing food for their families. Increases in women's nutritional knowledge help ensure better preparation, preservation, handling and distribution of foods. Increased capacity to handle their responsibilities can, in turn, enhance women's social and economic status. Thus, ensuring schooling with effective nutrition interventions for young girls can be one of the most important and effective means of improving women's nutrition and health status because of the associated effects on health, fertility and social development.

Healthy nutrition contributes to decreasing the risks of today's leading health problems

Studies show that early indicators of chronic disease begin in youth. For instance, avoiding obesity in childhood and youth is important because once attained, obesity tends to continue in adulthood, contributing to chronic diseases. Furthermore, the hardening of arteries and high blood cholesterol levels, which make a major contribution to coronary heart disease, are influenced by nutrition and lifestyle. Thus, adequate nutrition and physical activity are likely to have long-term health benefits in reducing the growing number of diet-related, non-communicable diseases.

— Obesity in infants, children and adults is a major problem worldwide. The prevalence of obesity in adults is 10% to 25% in most countries of Western Europe, 20% to 25% in some countries in the Americas, up to 40% in some countries in Eastern Europe, and more than 50% in some countries in the Western Pacific. Obesity rates, which are doubling every 5-10 years in many parts of the world, are placing significant additional financial burdens on health systems to deal with the resulting problems. Obesity will eventually lead to chronic disorders such as diabetes, high blood pressure, high cholesterol levels, hardening of arteries and some forms of cancer. Obesity also leads to acute consequences of chronic disorders including strokes and heart attacks. Reducing caloric intake and increasing physical activity help decrease the risk of obesity.

— Cardiovascular Diseases include coronary heart disease which is a major cause of adult death. The risk of cardiovascular disease can be decreased by healthy eating, especially by consuming a low fat diet.

— Cancer accounts for 25% of all deaths in developed countries. It has been suggested that practicable dietary means could reduce cancer deaths by as much as 35%. Eating a diet that contains plenty of fruit and vegetables in general can significantly reduce the risk of cancer.

— Eating Disorders present serious threats to adolescents' health and can lead to death. Psychological counselling, medical treatment and dietary advice can help to prevent and treat eating disorders.

Nutrition education has been shown to have a significant effect in fostering healthful eating habits. Thus, schools can contribute to reducing these nutrition-related problems by integrating nutrition interventions into a comprehensive approach to school health, as illustrated by the Health-Promoting School.

Education and good nutrition strengthen the economy

Adequate nutrition is necessary for children to become fit and productive adults, capable of fulfilling their responsibilities in life. People who are well-nourished and educated are clearly more productive and consequently improve their own income as well as their contribution to the national economy. For instance, improvements in health and wellbeing of women and their families through better nutrition contribute to reducing their financial burdens and time constraints. Gained time and resources can be used for income-generating and productive activities or for participating in educational, health or social engagements from which women and their families can benefit.

Furthermore, implementing essential public health programmes, including nutrition and health education and micronutrient supplementation, have been estimated to reduce a considerable amount of the disease burden in low- and middle-income countries. For example, using conservative assumptions, the benefits of investing in school feeding will far exceed the costs even though this is one of the most expensive possible nutrition interventions. In addition, nutrition interventions can contribute to reducing the substantial health care costs for nutrition-related chronic diseases and for productivity losses due to nutrition-related health problems.

Malnutrition weakens the learning potential and well-being of children

The education of millions of children throughout the world is being held back by malnutrition. Malnutrition in early childhood can affect school aptitudes, time of school enrolment, concentration and attentiveness. Children with a history of severe malnutrition perform less well on tests of IQ and specific factual knowledge than children in matched comparison groups. Undernourishment also impairs the ability to concentrate, learn and attend school regularly. A child who is malnourished and subsequently suffering from poor health cannot adequately take advantage of instructional and learning materials. Thus, good nutrition is needed to strengthen the learning potential of children, to enable them to learn effectively and maximise investments in education.

Malnutrition causes death and impairs the growth and development of millions of children

Malnutrition is a major factor in 54% of deaths to children under the age of 5 in the developing world. Moreover, 83% of these deaths are attributable to mild-to-moderate, rather than severe, malnutrition. Malnutrition disrupts growth and weakens the mental development of children, leading to less fit and productive adults. For example:

— Protein-energy malnutrition (PEM) affects about 200 million children worldwide under the age of 5. The actual numbers of protein-energy malnourished children has recently risen in Africa and South-East Asia. Protein-deficient children do not grow at their genetic potential. They also have an increased risk of severe consequences from common childhood infections. Current and prior protein-energy malnutrition has been shown to result in poor retention of factual knowledge, poor school attendance and poor school performance.

— Iron deficiency affects approximately 2 000 million people in developed and developing countries (16). Iron deficiency anaemia in infants and children can retard physical growth and delay cognitive development as well as increase susceptibility to infection. Furthermore, it impairs the reproductive function of women, which puts the lives of both · women and their babies at risk.

— Vitamin A deficiency puts over 250 million children worldwide at risk of blindness. Every year up to one half of a million children become partly or totally blind. Two-thirds of these children die within a few months of going blind. Even moderate levels of deficiency can lead to stunted growth, increased susceptibility and severity of infections and higher death rates. Vitamin A deficiency is the single greatest cause of preventable childhood blindness.

— Iodine deficiency is estimated to affect over 800 million people worldwide. Over 40 million people are affected by some degree of iodine deficiencyrelated brain damage. In later infancy and childhood, iodine deficiency causes mental retardation, delayed motor development, growth failure, stunting, speech and hearing defects. Iodine deficiency is the single most common preventable cause of mental retardation and brain damage in children.

All of these consequences of malnutrition compromise children's attendance and performance at school. They can be reduced by school-based interventions. Also, educating parents, parents-to-be and other family and community members as well as providing resources to correct deficiencies will help decrease the risk of developing these conditions.

Convincing Others that Nutrition Interventions in schools will really work

This section provides arguments that can be used to convince policy- and decision-makers and others of the effectiveness of nutrition interventions to promote health through schools. They also provide reasons to justify decisions to support such efforts.

Nutrition interventions improve children's health, learning potential and school attendance

Good health and nutrition are needed for concentration, regular school attendance and optimum class performance. Existing research makes a convincing case that nutrition and health interventions will improve school performance. For instance, studies in multiple countries show that the academic performance and mental ability of pupils with good nutritional status are significantly higher than those of pupils with poor nutritional status. This and other evidence of the positive impact of good nutrition has been so convincing that the United Nations Sub-Committee on Nutrition recommends health and nutrition programmes among efforts to increase school enrolment and learning.

Schools are vitally important settings through which to promote good nutrition and provide nutrition interventions

Schools offer more effective, efficient and equal opportunities than any other setting to promote health and healthy eating. They reach young people at a critical age of development in which lifestyles, including eating patterns, are developed, tested and adapted in schools and through social interactions between students, teachers, parents and others. Especially, lower grade levels provide excellent opportunities because eating habits are formed early in life. In addition, schools have the potential to reach not only students but also staff, teachers, parents and community members, including young people not attending school. A Health-Promoting School provides a means to develop and manage nutrition interventions in cooperation with parents and students.

Schools are an ideal setting to promote health and healthy nutrition for several reasons:

— Schools reach a high proportion of children and adolescents.

— Schools provide opportunities to practice healthy eating and food safety.

— Schools can teach students how to resist unhealthy social pressures since eating is a socially learned behaviour that is influenced by social pressures.

— Skilled personnel are available to provide follow-up and guidance - after appropriate training of students, teachers and other service personnel.

— Evaluations show that school-based nutrition education can improve eating behaviours of young persons.

We know how to improve health and well-being through school nutrition interventions

Evidence for many years has supported that well-managed nutrition education programmes can, at relatively low cost, bring about behaviour changes that contribute to improved nutritional well-being. For instance, studies in the United States have documented that carefully designed and implemented comprehensive health education curricula can prevent certain adverse health behaviours, including dietary patterns that cause disease. Students in behaviourally based health and nutrition education programmes have shown significant favourable changes in blood cholesterol, blood pressure and body fat. Thus, a focus on behaviour is considered a key determinant in the success of nutrition education programmes.

Additionally, school feeding programmes increase food availability to schoolchildren who need adequate food while promoting long-term development through support and education. While studies still continue, numerous evaluations of school feeding programmes have reported either significant increases in height and/or weight for participating children or in attendance and achievement. School feeding programmes also contribute to decrease hunger, which helps children concentrate on their studies.

Schools can provide interventions to improve nutrition in ways that are highly cost-effective

Cost-effective interventions in schools can prevent or greatly reduce health problems and consequences of malnutrition and foster the positive effects of nutrition. Compared with various public health approaches, school health programmes that provide safe and low-cost health service interventions, such as screening and health education, are shown by research to be one of the most cost-effective investments a nation can make to improve health. Furthermore, among the most cost-effective investments in health are programmes that include expanded micronutrient supplementation and increased knowledge about nutrition. Illustratively, a nutrition education programme in Indonesia which was based on behavioural change showed a considerably greater impact at notably lower cost than other types of interventions to which it was compared.

Education and healthy nutrition for girls have a positive impact on the health of families

Improving and expanding educational opportunities for girls is one of the best health and social investments. Improvements to girls' health will in turn improve the health of their children and families because women generally have a major responsibility to care for others within the household. This generally involves household management, food preparation, cleaning duties, obtaining health care, education and supervision of children, all of which can have a significant impact on health.

Furthermore, educated girls are healthier than girls with no or little education. Educated girls and women seek appropriate prenatal care, give birth to healthier babies and bring them home to healthier environments. Research evidence makes it clear that the single most important factor in determining a child's health and nutritional status is its mother's level of education. Malnourished mothers tend to have low birth weight babies, thus perpetuating the problem of malnutrition and ill health from one generation to the next. For instance, a child's aptitude for formal education may be in jeopardy even prior to school enrolment if the mother suffered from maternal iodine deficiency during pregnancy. Thus, educating young mothers and mothers-to-be is one of the best ways of ensuring the nutritional future of the next generation. In addition, the school system may be particularly useful in trying to supplement the diet of girls before puberty to ensure the remaining growth potential is fully achieved during this critical stage.

Nutrition interventions in schools benefit the entire community

School health education about good nutrition also serves as a means to inform families and other community members about ways to promote wellbeing and prevent malnutrition. For instance, educating children about good eating habits has the potential to enhance the nutrition and health status of their younger siblings whom they may take care of as well as of other family members that learn concomitantly with their children. In addition, involving parents in nutrition interventions at the elementary school level has been shown to enhance the eating behaviour of both students and parents.

Research also shows that school health education interventions can be considerably strengthened by complementary community-wide strategies. Thus, schools can be the centre for community enhancement projects that include programmes to improve the health and nutritional status of the community. Schools also provide a setting to introduce new health information and technologies to the community. For instance, the establishment of school canteens offering healthy food choices and practising good food safety is a way to demonstrate how to improve facilities in communities. Furthermore, partnerships between schools, organisations and businesses can benefit both the school and the community, if the partnership is mutually beneficial.

Interventions

Nutrition can be an entry point for building a school's capacity to plan and implement a wide range of health promotion strategies and interventions that will respond to identified needs and contribute to both health and education. Once nutrition is recognised as a priority for both education and health, the next step is to plan the interventions. This can be done by determining which strategies will have the most significant influence on health, education and development and how such interventions can be integrated with other health promotion efforts for maximum results. Interventions should enable students, parents, teachers and community members to make healthy decisions, practice healthy behaviours and create conditions conducive to health.

This section describes important steps that should be considered in planning healthy nutrition as an essential element of a Health-Promoting School. Steps include establishing or involving a school health team and a community advisory committee, conducting a situation analysis, obtaining political and community commitments, establishing supportive school health policies and setting objectives.

School and Community Involvement in Planning

Health-Promoting Schools involve members of the school and community in planning programmes that respond to their needs and that can be maintained with available resources and commitments. Two important groups that should be involved in the planning process are a school health team and a community advisory committee.

School health team

A Health-Promoting School should have a designated team to coordinate and monitor health promotion policies and activities. Since schools should implement programmes that respond to important and relevant community needs, it is essential to involve students, parents, teachers and school management from the beginning in the planning process. When young people are involved early, they can help develop and plan a programme that responds to their specific needs and concerns. Parents and teachers can help ensure that programmes are developed in a culturally appropriate manner. Active participation also builds a sense of ownership of the programme, which enhances its sustainability and support. Since teachers and other school staff play a key role in carrying out health promotion interventions, their participation is important to ensure that interventions are developed with consideration to what they know and what they can do to establish healthy nutrition as an essential element of a Health-Promoting School.

If a school does not have a committee or group organised to address health promotion, the healthy nutrition effort can provide the opportunity to form one. The team should include a balance of students and adults with various responsibilities in the school who are committed to the idea of health and healthy nutrition. Potential members of the school health team include: teachers, administrators, students, parents and school-based service providers, such as members of food services and health services. A school health team needs to be designated with responsibility and given time and authority to lead and oversee health promotion efforts in the school. A healthy nutrition task force within that group can be responsible for planning, designing and evaluating efforts to achieve healthy nutrition.

Community advisory committee

It is also important to work with groups and individuals outside of the school who have an impact on students' knowledge, attitudes and behaviours related to eating. If the school or school district has a community advisory committee, it is essential to find out whether they address health promotion and nutrition. If such a committee does not exist, implementing healthy nutrition provides an opportunity to form one or to identify community advisors who can work with the school health team to improve health and nutrition. In some settings it may be beneficial to collaborate with existing community groups, such as a healthy city council or school board.

Potential partners from outside the school include: representatives of local government, community residents, businesses, vendors, media, community youth agencies, nongovernmental organisations, social service providers, health service providers, sports figures and religious leaders. Subsequently, this committee can also address other health promotion issues.

To facilitate the efforts of the school health team, the community advisory committee, or selected advisors, can help determine local needs and resources, disseminate information about health and healthy nutrition, build support across the community, encourage community involvement, help to obtain resources and funding for health and nutrition interventions, and reinforce learning experiences provided in school. The committee should include men and women with a diversity of skills who are influential in the community or district, interested in health promotion and healthy nutrition, able to mobilise support and connections, and represent the community's geographical areas as well as economic, social, ethnic and religious makeup.

The community advisory committee and the school health team should work together in planning health promotion efforts and in coordinating the various components of a Health-Promoting School, such as health education, health services, community and family involvement, etc., so that all aspects of health promotion work together for health and healthy nutrition.

Situation analysis

A situation analysis should be considered by policy- and decision-makers and other interested groups at national, district and local levels to support the development of a Health-Promoting School and healthy nutrition. At the local level, once a school health team and community advisory committee or other responsible authorities are established, they can start planning interventions by conducting a situation analysis.

Purpose of conducting a situation analysis

Conducting a situation analysis will help people to better understand the needs, resources and conditions that are relevant to planning interventions. The necessity for an adequate situation analysis on a national, district and/or local school level is justified by several reasons:

— Policy- and decision-makers will need a strong basis for their support, especially when their policies and decisions involve the allocation of resources.

— Accurate and up-to-date data and information provide a basis for discussion, justification, setting priorities for action and identifying groups in special need for intervention, such as children belonging to underprivileged and minority groups or living in geographical areas where nutritional deficiencies are prevalent.

— Data obtained through the situation analysis are essential for planning and evaluating interventions. Data can help ensure that programmes focus on the actual health needs, experience, motivation and strengths of the target population so that interventions increase physical, social and mental well-being of students, staff, families and community members. Data also serve as a baseline to observe future trends in nutritional status and dietary behaviour.

Information needed

Various quantitative and qualitative information is needed for planning health promotion and nutrition interventions and for establishing a baseline for evaluation. Quantitative information includes numbers and scores while qualitative information includes perceptions and feelings.

The following information can help determine local needs concerning nutrition:

— Current health and nutritional status at national, regional, local and/or school level and how well it corresponds with relevant guidelines. This data should include the proportion of persons who are affected by malnutrition and infections and how severely they are affected.

— Knowledge, attitudes, beliefs, values, behaviours and conditions related to health and nutrition, eating patterns and food customs. For example, people might not know which foods are nutritious; poorly prepared food may influence a student's attitude about food that may be highly nutritious; local beliefs or superstitions may prevent people from eating certain foods; people might choose to ignore conditions of malnutrition because they have been with them for generations; or people might not be familiar with precautions to safely preserve food. This information is crucial to design effective health promotion strategies because values, beliefs and attitudes positively or negatively influence behaviours and conditions associated with nutrition and health. Without information about these helping or hindering forces, educational interventions are not likely to be targeted to the most relevant factors that contribute to health or malnutrition in the community and thus are unlikely to achieve the desired result.

— Available resources in the school and community. This includes determining which specific personnel and financial resources and services are available. Assessments should include the nature and extent of existing programmes, either through the school or community, that might help in implementing health promotion and nutrition interventions, such as deworming, oral hygiene or sport programmes. Knowing this information allows the school health team to draw on available resources for implementing new programmes or improving existing ones.

Commitment and Policies

Nutrition interventions in a Health-Promoting School are

most successful when a wide range of individuals and groups support the programme and become involved in it. It is important in the early stages to secure the acceptance and support of government officials, community and business leaders, educators, parents, students and the community in general.

Political commitment

National policies, guidelines and support from ministries of health, education, food and agriculture can be of immense help to local schools. Efforts to promote healthy nutrition through schools are most successful with the will, commitment, attention, support and action of these authorities. Collaborative relationships with other sectors and with local governments will also prove valuable.

Political commitment is evidenced by:

— Public acknowledgement by government officials of the importance of nutrition for health, education and development and the importance of providing nutrition interventions.

— Clear sanction and support from the ministries of education, health, food and agriculture for health promotion and nutrition interventions.

— Designation of someone with responsibility and authority at national, district and local levels to deal with health and nutrition issues and plan interventions.

— Financial support for school health promotion and nutrition interventions.

— Training, equipment and materials to enable schools to develop and implement health and nutrition interventions.

Community commitment

The success of efforts to create a Health-Promoting School relies also on the extent to which people in the community are aware of and willing to support health promotion efforts. Schools need to receive input from parents and community members regarding the design, delivery, content and assessment of school health promotion, so as to respond to their concerns and to attain their commitment. Family and community members should be involved very early; for instance, through community group meetings, parent-teacher associations, formal presentations, open houses, civic clubs and religious centres. Commitment and support of many parties on various levels is needed to share expertise, facilities and resources. Partnerships of representative individuals, groups and organisations from numerous sectors, such as nongovernment, education, health, business, agriculture, communication, recreation, voluntary service and religion can demonstrate and provide commitment, resources and support for health promotion and nutrition interventions.

Community commitment is strengthened/marked by.

— Public acknowledgement of the importance of healthy nutrition by community leaders and local health, education, agricultural and other relevant organisations and businesses.

— Establishment of a designated committee for coordinating community nutrition interventions.

— Provision of local resources for health and nutrition interventions in schools.

— Coordination of interventions with other programmes in the community (e.g. food supplementation programmes, farmers' support programmes, food safety efforts).

— Efforts to attract community and media attention (e.g. through printed material, community forums, tours of places that produce or process food).

Supportive school policies

Supportive school policies provide an essential framework that guides schools in planning, implementing and evaluating efforts to promote health and healthy nutrition. School policies are brief documents that promote a clear set of school norms regarding health and nutrition. They incorporate input from all relevant constituents of the school community: students, teachers, parents, staff, administrators, food service personnel, nurses and counsellors. Policies need to meet national and local needs and standards and should be adapted to the health concerns, food preferences and dietary practices of different ethnic and cultural groups represented at school. Policies that support collaboration and coordination between the health, education, food and agricultural sectors of the government and between the school and the community are encouraged.

Written policies should guarantee nutrition and other health interventions for all levels of schooling, starting in the earliest grade and continuing through the last grade. Policies should address all components of a Health-Promoting School that will be modified, such as education about nutrition, food choices at the school canteen, feeding programmes, family involvement and food handling procedures. Especially important are regulations about a Health-Promoting School's environment and about health education. For instance, school policies should guarantee adequate sanitation, a pleasant eating environment and collaboration with vendors as well as provision of teacher training, learning materials and a curriculum for nutrition and health education. Specific examples of supportive school policies include:

Regulations, rules and Protocols that Ensure

— ... students, parents, teachers and other school personnel are involved in planning of health promotion and nutrition interventions; for instance, through their participation on the school health team.

— ... the community advisory committee meets periodically to sustain coordination between school and community.

— ... the school curriculum includes education about nutrition as part of a sequential, comprehensive school health education programme, as an integral part of other relevant subject areas or, ideally, as a combination of both.

— ... teachers and other school personnel receive ongoing training about nutrition and food safety.

— ... all school facilities and events, including cafeterias, snack bars, rewards, staff meetings, parents' meetings and special events serve nutritious food, based on local, district and/or national guidelines.

— ... parents are educated about the value of healthy meals and food safety practices and about their role as reinforcers and motivators of concepts and knowledge for better eating and learning.

— ... school health services offer screening for conditions of malnutrition among students (where relevant) and report the results to teachers, parents and community members.

Goals and Objectives of Nutrition Interventions in Schools

Using the information gathered in the situation analysis, the school health team, in collaboration with the community advisory committee, can develop a vision for change and an action plan. This provides a basis for formulating goals and objectives for health promotion and nutrition interventions. Goals and objectives are necessary to make clear what the interventions should achieve. They are also essential to evaluate the extent to which the desired outcomes have been reached.

Goals

The goals should describe in broad terms what the programme will achieve. Nutrition intervention goals of a Health-Promoting School should aim at:

— gaining the full health and educational potential of food and nutrition sources for students and other members of the school, family and community.

— applying the school's full organisational potential to improve the nutritional status of students, staff, families and community members.

— laying a foundation of lifelong healthy eating based on favourable experiences, sufficient skills and confidence in one's capacity to practice a healthy lifestyle.

The goals are then broken down into specific outcome and process objectives so that everyone clearly understands what needs to be done, when and why. Objectives are steps for reaching the overall goal and describe outcomes in measurable terms that will help determine how successfully the goal is being reached.

Integrating Nutrition Interventions

A Health-Promoting School strives to use the school's full organisational capacity to improve the health of students, school personnel, families and community members. Such a school offers many opportunities to promote nutrition as an essential element for the attainment of health.

Nutrition interventions can serve as an entry point for the development or enhancement of policies, planning groups and various components which serve as a framework for a Health-Promoting School. These components include, but are not limited to:

— School health education - Community and family involvement and outreach

— Healthy school environment - Physical exercise, recreation and sport

— School health services - Counselling and social support

— Nutrition and food programmes - Health promotion for school staff

The effectiveness of interventions integrated into each of the above components is influenced by the extent to which they are supported by a variety of people, policies and trained staff. The effectiveness is also influenced by the extent to which interventions in each of these components combine with other health promotion efforts to complement and reinforce each other.

Not all schools will have the resources to integrate nutrition interventions into all of the components at one time. Therefore, each school has to establish its own priorities, in collaboration with all parties concerned, to decide the extent to which the components should be addressed. A Health-Promoting School enables students, parents, teachers and community members to work together to make such decisions. It is more important to start with small changes that are possible than to wait until resources become available to address all of these components simultaneously.

School Health Education

The primary goals of school health education are to help individuals adopt behaviours and to create conditions that are conducive to health. Thus, the clear and precise delineation of behaviours and conditions specifically relevant to healthy nutrition is essential for the development of effective school health education efforts. Examples of behaviours and conditions commonly identified with healthy nutrition are listed in Annex 3. These are not all inclusive, and national guidelines are available that provide advice relevant to individuals in specific countries. Close collaboration between education, health and food officials; the school health team; the community advisory committee; and other school and community members is necessary to identify the nutrition-related behaviours and conditions relevant to health in each community.

School health education is designed to help students acquire the knowledge, attitudes, beliefs and skills which are needed to make informed decisions, practice healthy behaviours and create conditions that are conducive to health.

— Knowledge provides a factual background on which to base decisions, such as knowledge about the relationship of eating and health and about planning for healthy nutrition using assessments and nutritional guidelines.

— Attitudes provide a personal perception for decisions, such as feeling responsible for one's own health and the health of others.

— Beliefs provide a conviction for decisions, such as a belief that healthy eating makes a positive difference in well-being.

3

Creating Healthy School Environment

A school's environment can enhance social and emotional well-being, and learning when it:

— is warm, friendly and rewards learning

— promotes cooperation rather than competition

— facilitates supportive, open communications

— views the provision of creative opportunities as important

— prevents physical punishment, bullying, harassment and violence, by encouraging the development of procedures and policies that do not support physical punishment and that promote non-violent interaction on the playground, in class and among staff and students.

— promotes the rights of boys and girls through equal opportunities and democratic procedures.

A healthy psycho-social environment simultaneously provides support to teachers, students and their families.

Psycho-social Environment

Research on work and home environments has shown that there can be a strong relationship between social settings and short and long-term emotional well-being. Considering how much time most children spend at school, psycho-social dimensions of schools have sparked the interest of a growing number of researchers concerned with school effectiveness and the emotional well-being of young people. Below are some conclusions from this research, with specific studies cited as supporting examples. Additional explanations about the importance of each quality area of the school's psycho-social environment are presented in Annex 3, "Worksheets for leading discussions of quality areas." These findings can help you convince others that using the PSE Profile as a way to assess and improve your school is a worthwhile effort.

Positive Social Environment at School can Influence the Behaviour of Students

A study of health behaviour among school-age children coordinated by WHO showed a strong and progressive relationship between indicators of "alienation" from school and health compromising behaviours among students from Australia and Wales. The relationship was most clear with smoking and alcohol misuse. The authors recommend not only school health education, but also changes to the school environment and ethos.

Similarly, a study of 12-18 year old students in public schools in Ohio, USA, found that "school connectedness," or the feeling of closeness to school personnel and the school environment, decreased the likelihood of health risk behaviours during adolescence, including cigarette use.

Positive Psycho-social Environment at School can Affect the Mental Health and Well-being of Young People

A sense of connectedness, good communication, and perceptions of adult caring have been shown to be related to a wide range of mental health outcomes. For example, a study of the impact of school "climate" on the well-being and mental health of children in the Czech Republic found that schools with a climate of confidence and respect among principals, staff, pupils and parents had the least number of negative characteristics, including general anxiety, school anxiety, emotional and psychosomatic balance, attitudes toward school, etc.

Gadin and Hammarstrom analysed the relationship between psycho-social factors in the school environment and pupils' health and sense of self-worth in a sample of Swedish pupils. They found that problems in relations with classmates were the most recurrent psycho-social factor associated with ill-health. Lack of self-control at school affected self-worth among girls, but not among boys.

Supportive School Environment can Improve Student Learning Outcomes

In Australia and the United Kingdom, factors like relationships between teachers and students in classrooms, opportunities for student participation and responsibility, and support structures for teachers, have consistently shown to be associated with student progress. MacIntosh theorises that "positive reactions to school may increase the likelihood that students will stay in school longer, develop a commitment to learning, and use the institution to their advantage". Thus, a positive, supportive climate at school can make a critical contribution to the academic achievement.

Psycho-social Environment (PSE)

The PSE Profile is a series of questions related to the psychosocial environment of your school. The questions are intended to: create awareness among teachers, managers and students about the importance of a healthy psycho-social environment at school; and help you identify the positive characteristics of your school's environment, and which characteristics you can improve.

The PSE Profile assesses conditions within the school, on the school grounds, at after-school activities and during travel between school and home. You are encouraged to use what you learn from the PSE Profile to engage the school and community in determining priorities, developing strategies and taking action.

The ultimate aim of using the PSE Profile is to identify and change conditions that can increase the school's capacity to be supportive and caring toward all those who work there, and to promote learning and development. Pupils and teachers are likely to be the principle beneficiaries. The advantages of a positive school environment can be greater well-being and happiness, an improved sense of belonging and better quality of life for those engaged with the organisation.

Indirectly, it may result in better levels of academic achievement. It can also alter some of the more negative aspects of school life by reducing bullying and harassment, injury, truancy and absenteeism. It has the potential to diminish stereotyping and prejudice, fear, anxiety, depression and loss of motivation. Furthermore, feelings of well-being during childhood provide sound foundations for positive health in later adolescence and adulthood; and students working in a supportive school environment where they feel a sense of attachment are more likely to respect their surroundings.

The psycho-social environment of a school depends to a large extent on the policies and attitudes of the school staff and the way schools are organised. The PSE Profile is a good opportunity to raise the awareness of teachers and staff about how they do or do not contribute to a positive school environment.

At a minimum, the PSE Profile is designed to help teachers assess the situation in their own school and to make any organisational changes that would assist in promoting an atmosphere friendly to girls and boys. However, the PSE Profile can have broad and longterm benefits if it is completed by a diverse range of school personnel, including administrators, cleaners, secretarial staff, volunteers, and, where applicable: playground monitors, cafeteria staff, the school nurse, and traffic safety patrol.

The selection of relevant participants will differ from school to school. Involving students can yield valuable insight about the school's psycho-social environment, since the perceptions of adults and young people are likely to differ. Although the PSE Profile is not designed for use by schoolchildren, it is important for teachers and others to include students (girls and boys) in discussions of items in the Profile that relate to the experience and perceptions of students. It is also important to involve students in discussions about the findings, and to include students in the implementation of any changes that may arise from the result (a complementary PSE Profile for students will be developed in the next phase of this project).

The number of persons who are asked to fill out the PSE Profile will vary from school to school. Small schools can invite all school personnel to respond. Large schools may wish to select a sample of school personnel, at random, to save time and effort. The table below shows the number of school personnel to include in a sample that would allow you to be 95 per cent sure that the responses are representative of all school personnel.

Number of employees in your school	*Suggested sample size*
50	38

100	73
150	96
200	115
250	129
300	141

The PSE Profile can be administered by any group that has been formed at the school to improve the quality of the school. For example, the administration of the PSE Profile could be coordinated by the School Health Team. If you do not already have such a team or similar group, Tool 1.1 in Local Action: Creating Health-Promoting Schools can help you form a diverse team of staff, students and community members with expertise and interest to work on issues relating to the health of the school community. The School Health Team can ensure that the PSE Profile and resulting actions are integrated with other health-related initiatives.

Involving a wide range of stakeholders, particularly teachers, school personnel and school and community leaders, in the administration of the PSE Profile can help you garner support when you are ready to implement the changes that the school agrees are necessary. For example, school and community leaders could be responsible for drafting new school policies through discussions with teachers, students and parents.

At a later stage, all the people who were involved in developing new school policies are likely to play a key role in supporting and promoting approved policies. They may wish to share the outcomes of any successful policy changes and actions so that other schools in the area can share and possibly benefit from their experience. Those responsible for administering the PSE Profile may wish to follow these suggested steps:

— Review the PSE Profile to become acquainted with the questions and determine if it needs to be adapted.
— Decide who should fill out the PSE Profile.
— Hold a meeting with all PSE Profile users to discuss the purpose of using it, clarify how the results will be used, and give the instructions for completing it.
— Tabulate the score of each completed PSE Profile and summarise the scores for all the PSE Profiles completed in your school.
— Circulate the results to all members of the school.
— Hold an open school conference to review the findings and plan actions for change.

A schedule for implementing these steps should be developed with consideration of other important efforts going on at the school, and within a time period short enough to maintain coherence, continuity and interest throughout the effort.

The PSE Profile requires the time of administrators, teachers and other school personnel. It also draws on other resources that are already available in the school. For this reason, this project is unlikely to require significant additional costs. It relies on the goodwill of the staff in the school-and others who assist them-to use the PSE Profile, discuss the results and plan and carry out changes that can be made at little or modest cost. This assessment is likely to highlight the need to reorganise or modify some practices or activities, rather than create new ones.

The issues addressed in the PSE Profile are common to many schools worldwide. Users are advised not to change or delete any parts of the Profile. However, there may be important factors or problems that are particularly relevant to schools in your system that are not necessarily shared by all education systems. We therefore invite users to consider whether they need to add questions to the PSE Profile before distributing it within their school. Those who decide to add new items should take care to justify their importance and relevance to the assessment.

Extra items should be phrased in the same style as the original PSE Profile items, using short unambiguous questions. All questions should be phrased so that they can be answered on the 4-point response scale used in the PSE Profile. Adopting this procedure will enable additional items to be scored in exactly the same way as the attached PSE Profile. We recommend that you minimise additional items so that the task does not become too burdensome and complex for users and administrators. Furthermore, it is important that the order of the questions in the PSE Profile itself is not changed in any way. Extra items should be added only at the end of the Profile.

Administrators of the PSE Profile are encouraged to write a brief introductory letter to accompany the Profile, explaining how the information that will be collected will be used. Administrators should also consider whether the Profile should be administered in a way that allows the respondent to remain anonymous, such as having completed Profiles returned to the administrator without names or other information that would identify the respondent; to do this may improve the accuracy of the results.

The questions in the PSE Profile are easy to score and the scoring procedure does not require the use of complicated statistics. Each question is scored on a scale from 1 to 4, with 1 representing the lowest and 4 the highest rating of social and emotional support. The total number of questions you answer will depend on whether your school is single sex or mixed boys and girls. Scores for single-sex schools can range from a minimum of 98 to a maximum of 392. Scores for mixed-sex schools can range from a minimum of 114 to a maximum of 456. To obtain an overall mean or average, simply add together all the scores for all the questions you answered and divide by the total number of questions answered.

4

School Health and Nutrition Programmes

In March 1990, world leaders gathered in Jomtien, Thailand, for the World Conference on Education for All: Meeting Basic Learning Needs. Its goal was to 'launch a renewed worldwide initiative to meet the basic learning needs of all children, youth and adults and to reverse the serious decline in basic education'. The conference organisers chose a different approach: rather than focus on the traditional issues of how to provide school buildings, textbooks, and teachers, they decided to address the process of learning and the needs of the learners. Health and nutrition were included as important contributors to the success of both the learner and the learning process.

In preparation for the round table, 'School Performance, Nutrition and Health' at the Conference, UNESCO published a key document - *Malnutrition and Infection in the Classroom* -which presented the relationship between the status of children's nutrition and health and their performance in school. The paper argued that because nutrition and health are so important in determining educational outcomes, they should figure prominently in any efforts to improve the quality of education and the ability of children to learn. In the preface, the Director-General of UNESCO stated, 'It is no longer possible to ignore the fact that nutrition and health can severely affect the ability of children to learn. We are constructing the future with the precious resource of the present - our children. It is essential that they be given the opportunity to derive maximum benefit from the schooling they receive'.

Schools have unique access to this 'precious resource'. In 1998, UNICEF estimated that out of 625 million children of primary school age, 79% were in school. The vast majority was receiving some basic education. It is also estimated that 70% of children in the developing world complete at least four years of schooling. Therefore, a school's potential to affect the health status and learning ability of an enormous number of the world's children stands before us. There are far more teachers than nurses or health-care workers in most countries. The teaching corps around the world can deliver many health promotion and health service interventions easily and effectively, with benefits to the teachers themselves as well. At the Jomtien Conference, participants echoed the need to broaden the perception of what contributes to basic education and to consider the many factors that affect human development.

They called for an expanded vision of basic education, one that recognised that 'education does not work in a vacuum or in isolation from other factors that have a bearing on society'. Ultimately, the 1990 World Declaration of EFA and its articles recognised the relationship among health, education, and health/ nutrition policies and programmes, stating that 'education can help ensure a safer, healthier, more prosperous and environmentally sound world' and learning does not take place in isolation.

Societies must ensure that all learners receive the nutrition, health care, and general physical and emotional support they need in order to participate actively in and benefit from education. To do so, new and revitalised partnerships at all levels will be necessary between education and social sectors.

Call for Action at Jomtien

Conference participants addressed the link between health and education. For example, UNESCO and the World Food Programme organised a round table on 'School Performance, Nutrition and Health'. The participants concluded that to learn effectively, children need good health. Further, they asserted that malnutrition and poor health may be important factors in low school enrolment, absenteeism, poor classroom performance, and early school drop-out.

The World Health Organisation and other agencies presented another round table, 'Health Education for All: Enabling School-age Children and Adults for Healthy Living'. The paper presented by WHO on this occasion contained a compelling call for action:

1. Health education must be inseparably linked with the Education for All initiative.
2. Countries must formulate and support clear policies on school health education and ensure that the education and health sectors have a joint strategy for their implementation.
3. Curriculum development must be based on the health needs of the different age groups and take into consideration the socio-cultural background of the schoolchildren. Curriculum development committees must include parents and community leaders.

4. Personal and social development must, along with intellectual development, be given due weight in schools in order to foster values, attitudes, and behaviour conducive to health and well-being.
5. The teaching of school health education requires teacher preparation, guidelines, teacher learning material and curriculum support. Teacher training institutions must revise their courses in the light of this need. Team training of all categories of school personnel, including the health, administrative, and general staff, is recommended for a comprehensive school health programme.
6. The pivotal role of teachers in promoting health in the school and community needs to be given high priority. The support of teacher associations must be sought to increase the health awareness of teachers and encourage them to assume responsibility for being role models for health in the school and community.
7. Schools must be health-promoting institutions. In addition to emphasis on the development and implementation of health education curricula, attention must be paid to ensuring that teachers and other staff and the school environment support and facilitate healthful living.
8. School health education must be planned and implemented in the context of the pupils' support, families and the wider community to which they belong. It must relate to the life of the child in and outside of school. Involving schoolchildren in community activities and the community in school activities will bring about greater understanding and encourage mutual support.

Although the round tables on school health and education gave strong and clear guidance for improving school health programmes as a means of achieving education for all, those recommendations were not given priority in the final report or in the Framework for Action following Jomtien. Furthermore, no specific goals for school health and nutrition or indicators were established for the decade 1990-2000.

Link between Learning and Health

In the decade since EFA, many publications and studies have elaborated on the link between learning and health status. A WHO report states, As long ago as 1950 it has been noted that nutritional deficiencies and poor health in primary-school-age children are among the causes of low school enrolment, high absenteeism, early dropout, and poor classroom performance. Health is thus a key factor in school entry as well as continued participation and attainment in school. Moreover, education that provides children with basic academic skills and specific knowledge, attitudes, and skills related to health is vital to their physical, psychological, and social well-being. This is not only true in the short term; such education lays the foundation for a child's healthy development through adolescence and across the entire lifespan'.

Education and Health are Inseparable

— Nutritional deficiencies (protein-energy malnutrition, iron, Vitamin A, and iodine deficiency) and health problems such as helminth infections (especially schistosomiasis and infections with roundworm and other intestinal parasites) and malaria affect school participation and learning. A 1990 analysis of nine studies on the relationship between nutritional anthropometric indicators (such as height-for-age and weight-for-height) and school indicators (such as age at enrolment, absenteeism, achievement test scores, IO and performance on selected cognitive tasks) showed that better nutritional status was consistently linked to higher cognitive test scores or better school performance.

— Violence, unintentional injuries, suicidal tendencies and related lifestyle behaviours, such as the use of alcohol and other drugs, interfere with the learning process. Children exposed to violence may become highly aggressive, use psychoactive substances, or show other dysfunctional ways of dealing with anxiety. This behaviour, in turn, may reduce attendance at school, impair concentration, and detrimentally affect cognitive development.

— Sexual behaviours, especially unprotected sex that results in HIV infection, other sexually transmitted diseases, and unwanted or too-early pregnancies, affect both students' and teachers' participation in education. These behaviours place at risk students who have successfully reached secondary school. Too-early pregnancies negatively affect the education of young girls, who often must drop out of school. HIV/AIDS has already had a devastating impact on children in sub-Saharan Africa, where over 90% of all AIDS orphans live - most of them will never complete a basic education.

It is important that most of these issues be addressed effectively through health, hygiene and nutrition policies and programmes for students and staff.

The Thematic Study on School Health and Nutrition explores what has happened in the field of school health and nutrition since 1990.

Effective strategies

Since Jomtien, a significant amount of research has been conducted on the effectiveness of school health interventions and the relationships between health, cognition, school participation, and academic achievement. This chapter presents highlights of the evidence to guide future investments in school health and nutrition.

The experience of the last decade has shown that if the quality and quantity of school health programmes are to increase, the education sector must take a leading role. Therefore, research data must be made easily available to the education sector and those committed to achieving EFA, to guide advocacy, policy development and programme planning. Ten major findings offer important guidance for the future:

1. School-based nutrition and health interventions can improve academic performance.
2. Students' health and nutrition status affects their enrolment, retention, and absenteeism.
3. Education benefits health.
4. Education can reduce social and gender inequities.
5. Health promotion for teachers benefits their health, morale, and quality of instruction.
6. Health promotion and disease prevention programmes are cost-effective.
7. Treating youngsters in school can reduce disease in the community.
8. Multiple co-ordinated strategies produce a greater effect than individual strategies, but multiple strategies for any one audience must be targeted carefully.
9. Health education is most effective when it uses interactive methods in a skills-based approach.
10. Trained teachers delivering health education produce more significant outcomes in student health knowledge and skills than untrained teachers.

Nutritional interventions such as micronutrient supplements and the treatment of intestinal worms have also proved to increase students' attention, cognitive problem-solving, and test scores. Research by the Ghana Partnership for Child Development showed that iron supplements - which could be effectively administered by teachers - lead to a very significant improvement in school performance for a period of up to six months. In Malawi, when the diets of primary-school children were supplemented with iron as well as iodine, the gain in IQ scores was greater than with iodine supplements alone. Two studies reviewed by Pollitt concluded that irondeficient anaemic children showed lower aptitude when they first enrolled in school. However, this disadvantage disappeared once the children became iron-replete. In the West Indies, a single chemotherapy treatment for whipworm infection given to children at school, without nutritional supplements or improvements in education, improved the children's learning capacity to the point that their test scores matched those of children who were not infected.

Students' health and nutrition status affects their enrolment, retention, and absenteeism

Height and weight for age are typical markers for entering school, and children not tall or heavy enough might be denied access. Thus, children in good health are more likely to start school at the developmentally appropriate age. 'For example, in Nepal, a study found that the probability of attending school was 5% for stunted children and 27% for children of normal nutritional status'. In Ghana, malnourished children entered school at a later age and completed fewer years of school than better-nourished children.

School feeding programmes have been shown to lower absenteeism and drop-out rates. A recent evaluation of a school feeding programme in Burkina Faso found that school food services were associated with regular attendance, consistently lower repeat rates, lower drop-out rates, and higher success rates in national examinations, especially for girls. In Malawi, a small pilot school-feeding programme over a threemonth period led to a 5% increase in enrolment and up to a 35% improvement in attendance. In the Dominican Republic, up to 25% of children - especially those from rural areas and girls - dropped out of school during a period without a school feeding programme.

Education benefits health

Regular school attendance is one of the essential means of improving health. The school itself - through its culture, organisation, and management; the quality of its physical and social environment; its curricula and teaching and learning methods; and the manner in which students' progress is assessed - has a direct effect on self-esteem, educational achievement, and therefore the health of students and staff.

Multiple years of schooling and the acquisition of literacy in several domains make it more likely that a person will be able to safeguard his or her health through living circumstances, earning power, access to health services, and general quality of life. Even a few years of schooling, evidence suggests, are associated with important changes of economic value in individual skills. Schooling pays off with higher incomes and a healthier workforce.

Education can reduce social and gender inequities

Poor health at school age is often connected with poverty and gender. School health programmes have the potential to reduce inequities in society and to begin to break the cycle of poverty. 'Poor children with the worst health have the most to gain from school-based health and nutrition programs and the most to gain educationally. They show the greatest improvement in cognition as a result of health interventions'.

During the twentieth century, 'education, skills and other knowledge have become crucial determinants of a person's and a nation's productivity. The primary determinant of a country's standard of living is how well it succeeds in developing and utilising the skills, knowledge, health, and habits of its population'. One major reason given for the dramatic differences in economic development between East Asia and Africa, for example, is the significantly higher level of investment that East Asia has made in the education and health care of its citizens. Thus, investments in education can have both short- and long-term benefits to an individual's health and the productivity of nations.

Girls, in particular, are likely to benefit: educated girls are likely to delay their first pregnancy and have fewer and healthier children. For example, data from thirteen African countries between 1975 and 1985 showed that a 10% increase in female literacy rates yielded a 10% reduction in child death rates. Schools are also places where girls' nutritional and reproductive health can be addressed early, thereby preventing later problems. In Tamil Nadur, a school feeding programme attracted more girls to attend school and improved the attendance of those already in school. In addition to benefiting educationally, these girls had the opportunity to learn about family planning. As a result they had fewer children when they reached child-bearing age'.

Health promotion for teachers benefits their health, morale, and quality of instruction

The health of teachers is an important factor in the learning process. Teachers are the key to both education and health promotion in schools. They are caretakers of both the school and the students. Their health is thus critical to the achievement of EFA. While teachers must be trained about health matters affecting students, they also need training about taking care of their own health. Inevitably, the physical and mental health of the staff affects students directly through the quality of teaching and the attributes of the school's psychosocial environment. Attending to teachers' health interests can motivate them to address students' health needs as well.

Some studies of the effectiveness of health promotion programmes for school staff have shown that they decrease teachers' absenteeism and improve both their morale and the quality of classroom instruction. Teachers who have participated in school health programmes reported improved attitudes towards their personal health and increased perceptions of general well-being. Other studies found that the school personnel's knowledge of and behaviours concerning health were positively affected. One staff programme in the United States demonstrated reductions in body weight, resting pulse rate, serum cholesterol level, and blood pressure.

Health promotion and disease prevention programmes are cost-effective

Money invested in the prevention of health problems through the schools can save societal costs of treating disease. A recent study in the United States estimated that every US dollar invested in schools on effective tobacco education saves $18.80 in the cost of addressing problems caused by tobacco use; every US dollar spent on education for preventing alcohol and other drug abuse saves $5.69; and every US dollar spent on education to prevent early and unprotected sexual behaviour saves $5.10.

A 1993 World Bank analysis determined that a basic publichealth package with five central elements could reduce the burden of disease for a relatively modest per capita cost. Extensive analyses of disease-control priorities have established that school-based treatments of children are exceptionally cost-effective. For example, school nutrition and health programmes have been estimated to cost only $20 to $34 per disability-adjusted life year (DALY) gained, and schoolbased tobacco and alcohol prevention programmes cost $35 to $55 per DALY gained.

Treating youngsters in school can reduce disease in the community

A leading publication by the World Bank, Class Action: Improving School Performance in the Developing World through Better Health and Nutrition, offers evidence that treating diseases prevalent in the school-age population can help to interrupt the transmission of disease to the surrounding community. For example, on the Caribbean Island of Montserrat, more than 90% of schoolchildren aged 4 to 12 were treated at four-month intervals for two and a-half months with an antiworm drug. Infection rates declined to almost zero. While less than 4% of adults in the community received treatment during the same time, their rate of infection declined an almost equal amount because of reduced transmission from the school-age children.

Multiple co-ordinated strategies produce a greater effect than individual strategies, but multiple strategies for any one audience must be targeted carefully

Strategies for school health programmes at both the national and local level have, for the most part, been singular in their approach. However, research continues to show the positive impact of multiple and targeted co-ordinated strategies. For example, a curriculum combined with youth community service is more effective in reducing risk behaviours such as fighting, early sexual behaviour, and substance use than a curriculum alone. Policies for tobacco-free schools, combined with a skills-based curriculum on tobacco prevention, are more effective than the curriculum alone.

In 1994 the Ghana Partnership for Child Development implemented a programme to treat parasitic infections in children through many schools in the Volta region. The programme used a combination of strategies, including clinical treatment, teacher and administrator training, and classroom education. After six months, test results showed a reduction in the prevalence of schistosomiasis from 15% to 5.7% and in hookworm from 52% to 2.4%. A re-survey in 1996 showed the prevalence of schistosomiasis to be 5.4% compared with 15.2% in 1994, and hookworm at a rate of 28% compared with 51% in 1994. In addition, children who took part in the programme improved both their attendance and school performance records.

Often there are not enough resources and time to accomplish all the goals of a health promotion or disease prevention effort. Programme planners must then choose between providing a variety of strategies for a given population or focusing on a smaller number of activities. The National Structured Evaluation of Alcohol and Drug Abuse Prevention in the United States undertook an analysis of more than 300 community-based substance abuse prevention initiatives. The researchers concluded that projects that attempted to offer more than three or four types of activity to a single adolescent population were generally ineffective. The study concluded that comprehensive prevention depends more on selecting appropriate activities and services for each population served than on trying to provide a wide variety of activities and services. There may be an effective limit to the variety of preven-tion activities that should be provided at a given time to a single population, beyond which the addition of a greater variety of activities adds little to measured effects of the prevention efforts'. The implication for school-based prevention is that planners need to select and target a few strategies to promote health, and to address the most serious health threats.

Health education is most effective when it uses interactive methods in a skills-based approach

Health education aims not only to improve pupils' interest in health, their ability to relate what they learn to their own lives, and their understanding of basic ideas about health, but also to apply what they learn to the lives of their families and friends. To do so, health learning must emphasize skills development over simple information sharing, and provide opportunities for students to practice healthy behaviours or to address the conditions that promote health both personally and collectively.

Skills-based health education, including life skills, and interactive teaching methods have been shown to promote healthy lifestyles and reduce risk behaviours. A meta-analysis of 207 school-based drug-prevention programmes grouped the approaches to prevention into nine categories. The author found that 'the most effective programs teach comprehensive life skills'. Programmes were also grouped according to whether they used interactive methods or not. The study concluded that 'the most successful of the interactive programs are the comprehensive life skills programs that incorporate the refusal skills offered in the social influences programs and add many general life skills such as assertiveness, coping, communication skills, etc.'

Skills-based health education and life skills have been shown to reduce the chances that young people will engage in delinquent behaviour and interpersonal violence; the use of alcohol, tobacco, and other drugs; high-risk sexual activity that can result in pregnancy or STD or HIV infections; emotional disorders; and bullying.

Trained teachers delivering health education produce more significant outcomes in student health knowledge and skills than untrained teachers

Training for school personnel is an important aspect of school health-promotion programmes. Studies show that training teachers how to use a health-education curriculum improves its implementation. Similarly, an evaluation of the Teenage Health Teaching Modules (THTM) curriculum, using skills-based approaches for health education in grades 7 to 12 in the United States, showed that training teachers before using the curriculum positively affected teachers' self-reported feeling of preparedness and had positive effects on both curriculum implementation and student outcomes. Students in health education classes taught by trained teachers scored significantly higher on health knowledge and attitude scores, and, at the senior high-school level, were also more able to curb self-reported use of illegal drugs, than those covering the same material with untrained teachers.

Training teachers has the added value of gaining their commitment and support, as well as their understanding of a specific curriculum and its supporting policies and programme - all important factors for successful implementation.

Moving from Research to Action

The effect on education of health issues, such as safe water and sanitation, helminth infections and nutrition, and lifestyle behaviours associated with STDs, HIV/AIDS, and alcohol, tobacco and other drugs are highlighted, and evidence is given that schools can address these issues effectively. Table II provides an overview of illustrative roles that educators and their collaborators can play to address selected health issues.

This research and the directions it suggests must be made more accessible to educators in order to make greater strides in the next decade to improve the health and education of the world's children. State-of-the-art knowledge must move from the pages of technical journals to discussions and debates in ministries, school buildings, classrooms, and communities. Only when these findings and ideas become part of daily conversations among administrators, teachers, and health workers will more attention be given to these important aspects of successful learning. Improvements in education will not succeed if we do not simultaneously pay attention to the healthy development of both students and staff in schools.

Suggestions for EFA 2015

With the research findings of the past ten years as a guide, the forthcoming decade shows great promise for strengthening the links between health and education. The record of the past decade affirms that the world community can translate its highest aspirations for children into effective programmes. If the past is indeed a prelude to the future, we can say with confidence that the pace in responding to the learning and health needs of children greatly accelerates once consensus has been achieved on policies and programmes that work. We hope that the following suggestions will encourage consensus on what countries must do to meet the health and learning needs of their school-age citizens. These suggestions emphasize the development of a shared vision, a commitment to act, a pledge to work collaboratively, and the importance of a global effort to acquire and share information.

Major leaders and change agents in the field must come together around a common framework, relevant to the education sector

Such a framework should be part of a larger effort to improve the general quality of the schools and the education children receive. The creation of frameworks in the past decade contributed enormously to driving the school health agenda forward. Frameworks have increased creativity, generated experimentation, and inspired a broad range of research and programme activities. At this juncture, however, we run the risk of allowing the proliferation of so many frameworks to diffuse human and financial resources and to confuse those who are ready to take action. A shared framework should drive an action agenda that:

1) promotes healthy development and focuses on the most serious and common health threats through the co-ordinated implementation of core components of a school health and nutrition programme in schools everywhere;
2) sets specific, quantifiable goals for the agenda;
3) applies lessons learned from the past decade on how best to implement the core components; and
4) establishes indicators to monitor the implementation and effectiveness of the core components in countries and schools worldwide.

A shared framework must view the school as a dynamic system in which people can effect change to promote health and learning and which focuses not only on children but also on staff, teachers, parents and community members, and links to health services.

To be successful, school health, hygiene and nutrition efforts must be led by educators, supported and assisted by health professionals, and made an integral part of the efforts to improve education through policies and goals

School health and nutrition efforts can have a powerful

effect on improving the status of schools (through efforts by schools and communities) as well as of education (through policies and goals). Much of the power of school health programmes lies in their ability to mobilise schools and communities around the improvement in educational quality and outcomes for their children. Educators must be convinced that such programmes are practical and feasible, yield results, are beneficial to staff and students, and advance learning. It is equally important that leaders relate the efforts to the social and economic agenda in gaining support. Recruiting a small but highly influential group of well-known and respected international educators to champion the school health agenda would be valuable.

We must continue to deepen and expand collaboration, especially between the education and health sectors, with mechanisms that sustain and nurture joint planning, action and learning over time

Experiments have taken place at the world, regional, and national levels to bring the education and health sectors together. Where successful, these collaborations have created a common language, provided unique contributions for sharing and learning, and leveraged resources. However, sustaining the collaboration is difficult. It is also important to identify and use the unique roles of various participants. Collaboration does not mean that everyone does the same thing, but that each sector makes its own unique contribution to common goals. Successful collaboration must identify the most relevant role for the educator, the health worker, and the parent and community member. More must be done to sustain emerging networks for collaboration, providing professional development, resources, and materials to increase their capacity and to sustain energy and commitment in the face of obstacles.

More investment is needed for health services that children and adolescents can reach easily, without stigma

More health services should be located in or near schools and staffed with people trained to work with youth. Young people all over the world need health services, particularly those that are 'youth-friendly'. Traditional health services must move beyond medical treatment to preventive services and early intervention and accommodate the particular needs of young people (e.g. for emotional support, confidentiality and accessibility).

Access to information as well as sustained support to use it (e.g. professional development, technical co-operation, and mentoring) must be improved for education and health workers

Much is known about the effectiveness of various school health and nutrition programmes. Research findings could have a much greater impact if they were accessible to more people. We must try to extract key findings from the many excellent technical documents that exist, and make them available in simple, clear formats and multiple languages for practitioners. There is a need for ongoing professional development and technical know-how for education and health workers about how to identify, select, and implement the most effective strategies for their needs. A creative use of the Internet and on-line training must be applied to the field of school health and nutrition on a global scale.

Multiple targeted and co-ordinated strategies are needed to improve desired behaviour patterns and health outcomes.

Research in public health, the foundation of most approaches to school health, has demonstrated that multiple strategies co-ordinated to address a few common goals are more effective in producing desired behaviour changes and health outcomes than single-track approaches. Such strategies may include co-ordinated policy, supportive environments, community action, personal skills, and health services targeted to a few selected conditions.

Indicators that provide universal measures of progress are needed to focus efforts and report changes that can be achieved by 2015

While there has been tremendous progress since Jomtien, it is impossible to tell the full story of what has happened globally without common indicators of progress. Such indicators could provide information about national capacities and infrastructure to implement school health programmes. Measures could include the availability of school policies and budgets with line items dedicated to health, mechanisms for collaboration, and the health-related training of teachers and health workers. Beyond measures of capacity, indicators of children's health status could include height and weight data, rates of anaemia and other micronutrient deficiency diseases, and number of meals or fruit and vegetable servings per day. At the national and local level, too, more and better programme planning and evaluation tools are necessary.

Model programmes should be developed for different levels of investment, because countries vary in what they can afford

We should identify the best package of inputs and services at different investment levels (e.g. $2, $5, and $10 per child). For each 'model package', we should also identify the expected benefits as precisely as possible. Such an approach will allow countries to launch school health initiatives that are both efficacious and affordable.

Another observation must inform our efforts in the future. In many countries, people who are very poor and disenfranchised have reported that their participation in addressing health issues in schools has made a difference to their lives. The opportunity to have a voice and role in creating change to improve the quality of life for their children, themselves, and their community has transformed their world. In his book Development as Freedom, the Nobel prizewinner for economics Dr Amartya Sen argues that reductions in poverty and progress in economic development are possible only when citizens have the freedom or opportunity to receive basic education and health care. With the participation of all - the education and health sectors, parents, teachers, and community members - people everywhere can make gradual improvements in their quality of life.

As we consider the changes that policy-makers, practitioners, and citizens can bring about in the future, it is good to reflect on developments in the past. The following chapters look back at the status of school health leading up to Jomtien in 1990, describe conceptual frameworks that were developed in the 1990s, and highlight major trends that took place in the field of school health and nutrition since Jomtien.

Historical perspective

International collaboration in school health has a history of more than 120 years. In the 1800s, school health became an issue when compulsory education laws were enforced in Europe. In 1880, the Third International Congress on Education in Brussels addressed school hygiene as one of the plenary topics. Through each decade of the 1900s, the agenda of international school health conferences included such topics as school construction and furniture, medical inspection in schools, individual health records, physical education and training, the hygiene of dormitories, the prevention of contagious diseases in schools, and hygiene for teachers, students, and families.

Following a 1946 survey of ministries of education, the International Bureau of Education of UNESCO prepared recommendations to improve the teaching of health in primary schools, with the goal of making it a genuine part of education. By 1967, all of the ninety-four countries replying to a second survey indicated that some form of health education was compulsory in primary schools and was often integrated into other subject areas, such as science education. Nevertheless, the report recognised that not all schools were effectively assisting children in adopting positive attitudes and behaviours about safeguarding their own health and that of others.

From the 1960s until the mid-1980s, international conferences and publications in the field of school health were less evident. This decline of attention at the international level was consequential because international leadership and advocacy can be catalytic for national and local efforts. However, during this same period when school health was less visible on the international stage, the developing world was making considerable progress on another front: increasing the survival rates of children from birth to 5 years of age. In 1960, only five of every six children born (83%) lived to their first birthday. By 1991, at least 12 of every 13 children born (92%) were expected to reach that landmark. The success of the Child Survival movement meant that more and more children were going to enter school. An important question began to emerge: how can we maintain and improve children's health to maximise their learning?

By the end of the 1980s, a number of international organisations renewed their interest in school health and nutrition programmes around the globe. UNESCO was one of the first United Nations agencies to address the area of school health and nutrition. In the 1980s, UNESCO initiated the Nutrition Education Series and held various technical meetings on this topic. Also, the Council on Europe, the European Commission, and the WHO Regional Office in Copenhagen were beginning to discuss a broader concept of school health. These groups looked at all aspects of the school as a system and a setting in which health could be promoted by those in it. In the United States, with the support of the Centers for Disease Control and Prevention, and backed by the evaluations of several major school health education programmes, the concept of a comprehensive school health programme with eight components became more widely understood and implemented.

As the 1980s came to a close, researchers around the world were beginning to evaluate the effectiveness of specific health interventions to address nutritional deficiencies and the treatment of intestinal worms, in particular, and, where possible, to examine the relationship of health interventions to cognition, school attendance, and other factors in learning. For example, in 1989 an examination of the global distribution of parasitic worm infections revealed that large parasitic burdens, particularly severe hookworm infection, were associated with impaired cognitive function as well as poor educational outcomes, such as absenteeism, under-enrolment, and attrition.

With these realities in mind, the Background Document for the World Conference on Education for All argued that 'the education sector needs to attend to the health needs of children or they may be rendered "unteachable"'. It went on to say that 'the adverse effects of malnutrition and poor health on education may indeed be jeopardising children's readiness to enter school, their ability to learn, and the duration of their schooling. Addressing children's nutrition and health could make a difference in terms of improving educational performance'.

Status of School Health in 1990

While there was growing recognition of the need to

address the health status of young people to maximise learning leading up to Jomtien, what was actually happening in school health policy and practice? Based on a synthesis of experts' reflections and published studies, school health efforts in 1990 can be characterised in the following ways:

1. Health initiatives in schools focused primarily on disease prevention.
2. There was confusion about the concept and definition of school health.
3. Single, uncoordinated intervention strategies dominated.
4. Few formal mechanisms for multisectoral collaboration were in place.
5. Didactic, topic-by-topic teaching was the typical approach to health education.
6. Evidence of the effectiveness of interventions was not well known or disseminated.
7. Few tools were available to guide assessment and strategic planning.
8. Few donors earmarked school health programmes as a priority for funding.

Health initiatives in schools focused primarily on disease prevention

Many school health efforts aimed to improve hygiene, prevent the spread of infections, treat specific health conditions, and provide screening or medical examinations. Many countries also expanded their efforts to incorporate health topics into national curricula. Both the services and curricular work tended to emphasize specific disease prevention more than health promotion.

For example, in 1987 Pakistan initiated a School Health Services Programme and recommended in its five-year plan that all children have a complete medical check-up when they enter school and a comprehensive quarterly check-up as long as they remain in school. Pakistan's subsequent five-year plan recommended that the programme be reoriented towards developing healthy lifestyles among schoolchildren, thus recognising the need for a more comprehensive and lifestyle-oriented approach. In 1990 Namibian schools provided immunisation, physical examinations, and a limited amount of information on 'health matters'. There were no policy guidelines, no provision for family-life education for either teachers or pupils, and the use of life skills education was just beginning.

In 1990 health and education professionals usually defined school health and nutrition as either health curriculum or health services, but seldom as the integration of the two. While the importance of linking health instruction to services and other components was often discussed, there was no unifying concept to galvanise all the participants to work together for a truly global effort. Experience has shown that a powerful concept can create enthusiasm and motivate policy-makers and practitioners to implement new ideas. And, as David Rivett of the European Network of Health-Promoting Schools said, 'It has been critical for us in Europe to have a concept or framework in place first. We have seen how the framework has driven the agenda and provided a map for action in countries and with local schools'.

In 1990, at the international level, there was no single, clear definition or framework across all the agencies to guide their direction and activity. In the early 1990s a few more integrated concepts began to appear. However, no matter what concept was used, school health and nutrition were often regarded as separate and apart from the mission of basic education. School health advocates often found themselves frustrated and unable to convince educators of the importance and interdependence of health and education.

Single, uncoordinated intervention strategies

In 1990, and in some cases to this day, the field of school health and nutrition depended primarily on single, uncoordinated strategies, which alone have limited potential for success. Many school health efforts involved curricula that were not complemented by policies or a supportive school environment. For example, teaching about the dangers of tobacco took place in schools in which students and faculty were allowed to smoke.

Similarly, health services treated conditions like intestinal worms, but often without complementary improvements in sanitation and safe water or educational messages to prevent re-infection. Seldom were approaches comprehensive, that is, uniting policy with instruction, services and the school environment to reinforce one another in targeting specific health and educational outcomes.

Sheldon Shaeffer of UNICEF, who worked extensively in East Asia, commented, 'Most of the activities which I saw were limited to putting water supply and latrines into schools. There may also have been a health education programme in the same school, but it was not co-ordinated with any other component of a school health programme. The water and sanitation effort was not accompanied by any reinforcing education strategy and there was no evaluation of academic outcomes. There was no look at whether the provision of these services increased enrolment or general use of the facilities by students or community members'.

Too often there has been a vertical approach to a problem such as malaria. For example, medical personnel will arrive at a school with the view that 'malaria is your problem and this is what you must do to treat it'. There has been little attempt to gain community participation and support for the intervention. Therefore its acceptance and success are limited. On the other hand, multiple strategies that are co-ordinated to address a few common goals have proved effective. In the United States, for example, Project Northland is a school/community substance-abuse prevention programme that includes planned parental involvement, peer-led skills-building sessions, community policy change and enforcement, all designed to test the efficacy of a multilevel, multistrategy, multiyear intervention programme for youth. After three years, an evaluation demonstrated that the percentage of students who reported alcohol use in the previous month and week was significantly lower in the intervention group at the end of eighth grade than in the reference group.

Few formal mechanisms for multisectoral collaboration

In 1990 there were few cross-sectoral mechanisms in place at the international, regional, national, or local levels. These mechanisms provide a way for partners to unite around common goals, co-ordinate and leverage valuable resources, provide a forum for learning, and exchange technical expertise. However, the education sector typically handled health instruction while the health sector addressed services, with few linkages between the two. Agencies responsible for water, sanitation, sanitation, and the school's physical structure have usually acted independently of the other sectors.

Given the effectiveness of targeting multiple strategies to improve children's health and learning, collaboration is necessary across sectors (education, public health, medicine, environmental services) and between agencies with common goals and interests (governmental and non-governmental agencies, national and international organisations). The lack of such important structural mechanisms to expedite policy development and programme implementation, combined with confusion about a unifying concept, was the most critical obstacle to progress in the field. Without such structures, it is difficult at any level to harness the multidisciplinary expertise and resources necessary to achieve school health goals.

Didactic, topic-by-topic teaching was the typical approach to health education

Most school health education programmes have been concerned with providing information on specific topics, not with building skills. A review of curricula from the early 1990s reveals that they typically provided information about ten topics, almost all about physical health or specific diseases, rather than building skills to practice healthy overall behaviour. Sexuality was usually omitted, as was any attention to emotional or mental health; violence and suicide were not regarded as public health issues.

A review of school health education in Europe in 1991 reported, 'There is general agreement in Europe over the range of health issues which need to be addressed in schools. There has been a tendency, however, for school health education to be dominated by single health issues - particularly drugs and AIDS - which has inhibited the whole-hearted adoption of the holistic healthy lifestyle approach necessary for a balanced and convincing programme in schools'.

While several innovative skills-based or life skills curricula were developed during the 1980s, the primary teaching method continued to be the didactic lecture. It has now been well documented that the teaching methods with the strongest likelihood of producing change in the health behaviour of students are interactive learning strategies or experiential learning.

Many in the field recognised the child-to-child approach as an outstanding programme in health education at the time of EFA. Begun in London, the child-to-child approach focused on teaching older children to deliver health messages to their younger siblings through interactive methods. Gradually, the approach expanded to prepare children to promote good health among their peers, families, and communities. Child-to-child placed young people in an active teaching role.

Evidence of the effectiveness of interventions

Few evaluations were made of the effectiveness of health education curricula or any other school health initiative. Those that did exist were disseminated primarily to health education professionals rather than to the mainstream education sector or to professionals in the public health or medical arenas. Similarly, research about health service interventions was published primarily in journals aimed at the medical, nutrition, or public health sectors. There were few opportunities for the two important audiences of educators and health workers to learn together about the important link between health and education. By 1990 a new body of research was emerging concerning the impact of health interventions on the status of health and on cognition and learning outcomes. But the findings were not widely disseminated. At the time, the Internet was in its infancy, and the dissemination of information, especially for developing countries, still relied almost exclusively on expensive printed documents, most often available only in English.

Tools for guide assessment and strategic planning

Planning in public health, education, and organisational development often begins with the collection of data to define the problem and the assets or strengths to address it. From there, planners can set measurable goals and objectives, then define action steps and milestones to measure progress. In 1990 few, if any, assessment and strategic planning tools were available for education policy-makers and programme planners to collect and use data to plan policies, programmes, and interventions in an integrated and complementary manner designed for the health needs of children and adolescents in school. Thus, educators in particular had little information about the strengths and limitations of the many parts of a school health programme that could have guided them in selecting and developing effective intervention strategies. In addition, there was limited information about the costs associated with implementing specific interventions.

Few donors earmarked school health programmes as a priority for funding

Many workers in the field share the general perception that it was difficult to find departments within United Nations agencies and international non-governmental organisations with a brief that included school health programmes. It was also difficult to find donors who had made it a priority to fund international efforts to improve school health programmes. The field of school health and nutrition has progressed considerably over the past decade.

Conceptual Frameworks: The Principles that Drive Action

A major accomplishment since the World Conference on Education for All in Jomtien has been the development of conceptual frameworks or unifying principles for school health policies and programmes. These frameworks have also served as a catalyst to mobilise partnerships across sectors at all levels. In addition to the frameworks developed by United Nations agencies and a few other international organisations, significant and noteworthy activity was also conducted by frontline grass-roots organisations in the past decade.

This chapter describes some of the major conceptual frameworks that have influenced the school health and nutrition agenda over the past decade. Frameworks developed in the 1990s include the concept of the Health-Promoting School; the Child-Friendly School (UNICEF); the Basic Cost-Effective Public Health Package (World Bank and the Partnership for Child Development, University of Oxford); and Active Learning Capacity. One framework, FRESH (Focusing Resources on Effective School Health, was launched jointly at the EFA Conference in Senegal in April 2000.

Framework of the Health-promoting School

The concept of the health-promoting school (HPS) started in Europe. It is based on public health theory and builds on the Ottawa Charter of Health Promotion, which recognised that 'health is created and lived by people within the settings of their everyday life; where they learn, work, play and love. Health is created by caring for oneself and others, by being able to make decisions and have control over one's life and circumstances, and by ensuring that the society one lives in creates conditions that allow the attainment of health by all its members' The WHO Regional Office for Europe, the Council of Europe, and the European Commission first widely promoted the HPS concept.

The aim was to achieve healthy lifestyles for the total school population by developing environments conducive to the promotion of health. The HPS concept extended beyond school health education to a broader array of complementary interventions. The earliest descriptions of the HPS, then called the 'Healthy School', were developed during the first major conference of all the European nations on school health promotion in Scotland in 1986. The model, described in a report by Young and Williams, featured an overarching policy and three essential co-ordinated components: instruction, health services, and a healthy school environment - both physical and psychosocial. A similar concept, the Eight Component Model, was developed in the United States by Allensworth and Kolbe in an effort to explore whether the concept of the school health programme should be expanded. If co-ordinated, the following eight components of the model could have complementary, if not synergistic, effects:

— school health services
— school health education
— school health environment
— integrated school and community health promotion efforts
— school physical education
— school food service
— school counselling
— school health-promotion programmes for faculty and staff

In the 1990s both of these frameworks guided many policy decisions and programming efforts throughout Europe and the former Soviet Union and in the United States. As documents and programme descriptions were published, interest grew among international and national health and education workers to apply them to the needs of a broad range of countries.

To gain a thorough understanding of the status of school health worldwide and prepare recommendations for improving health through schools, in 1994-95 WHO convened an Expert Committee. The Education

Development Center synthesised the findings from hundreds of evaluation research and feeder papers written by WHO staff and experts around the world. This initiative produced the following four documents, published by WHO: The Status of School Health; Improving School Health Programmes: Barriers and Strategies; Research to Improve Implementation and Effectiveness of School Health Programmes; and Promoting Health through Schools.

The Expert Committee concluded that research in both developing and developed countries demonstrates that school health programmes can simultaneously reduce common health problems, increase the efficiency of the education system, and further public health, education, and social and economic development in all nations. The committee made ten recommendations to improve health through schools worldwide.

Following the Expert Committee meeting and report in 1995, WHO launched its Global School Health Initiative to support schools to become Health-Promoting Schools. Although definitions will vary between regions, countries, and schools according to need and circumstance, an HPS can be characterised as a school that is constantly strengthening its capacity as a healthy setting for living, learning, and working.

A Health-Promoting School:

— Strives to improve the health of school personnel, families, and community members as well as students.

— Fosters health and learning with all the measures at its disposal.

— Engages health and education officials, teachers, teachers' unions, students, parents, health providers, and community leaders in efforts to make the school a healthy place.

— Strives to provide a healthy environment, school health education, and school health services along with school/ community projects and outreach, health promotion programmes for staff, nutrition and food safety programmes, opportunities for physical education and recreation, and programmes for counselling, social support, and mental health promotion.

— Implements policies and practices that respect an individual's well-being and dignity, provide multiple opportunities for success, and acknowledge good efforts and intentions as well as personal achievements.

The strategies have been implemented in collaboration with other relevant programmes and departments within WHO, including the WHO Regional Offices, and with international agencies that are interested in the development of Health-Promoting Schools, including Education International (EI), a professional organisation of about 25 million teachers worldwide, and the Child-to-Child Trust. The European Network of Health-Promoting Schools, for example, has since 1990 enrolled more than 500 pilot schools with 400,000 students in thirty-seven countries in Europe and the former Soviet Union.

Framework of the child-friendly school

Based on the Jomtien documents and a number of other developments in the field of children's rights, UNICEF has recently developed a framework of rights-based, childfriendly education systems and schools that are characterised by being 'healthy for children, effective with children, protective of children, and involved with families and communities - and children'.

This framework builds on the proclamation at the Jomtien Conference that 'education is a fundamental right for all people, women and men, of all ages, throughout our world'.

Referring to health, the declaration went on to say that 'education can help ensure a safer, healthier, more prosperous and environmentally sound world'.

UNICEF's framework was also inspired by the Convention on the Rights of the Child, held in 1989, which set the stage by acknowledging that children's rights require special protection for the purpose of the general improvement of their conditions and for their development and education.

UNICEF's framework broadly defines core components that characterise a child-friendly school, each component incorporating factors concerning education, health, and human rights. In a child-friendly school:

— The school is a significant personal and social environment in the lives of its students. A child-friendly school ensures every child an environment that is physically safe, emotionally secure, and psychologically enabling.

— Teachers are the single most important factor in creating an effective and inclusive classroom. Child-friendly schools are teacher-friendly, supporting, encouraging, and they facilitate teachers towards being motivated, capable, self-confident, and consistently available.

— Children are natural learners, but the capacity to learn can be undermined and sometimes destroyed. A child-friendly school recognises, encourages, and supports children's growing capacities as learners by providing a school culture, teaching behaviours, and curriculum content that are focused on learning and the learner.

— The ability of a school to be and to call itself child-friendly is directly linked to the support, participation, and collaboration it receives from families.

— Child-friendly schools have a key role to play in ensuring that children's rights are reflected throughout the education system, just as education systems must ensure that schools have the resources to act on behalf of all children.

— The rights of children as articulated in the CRC are indivisible. They all apply, all of the time, to all children. Schools and education systems have a role in ensuring that children's rights are reflected throughout a country's governance community. Child-friendliness is a broad public-policy matter.

Child-friendly schools aim to develop a learning environment in which children are motivated and able to learn. Staff members are friendly and welcoming to children and attend to all their health and safety needs. WHO supports the framework of the child-friendly school by helping schools become 'healthpromoting' as an essential step towards becoming 'childfriendly'.

Framework of the basic cost-effective public-health package

The concept that schools are in a position to deliver a basic package of health services to students has been widely acknowledged during the 1990s. The appropriate level of services for the schools to offer depends on each country's operational and financial resources. A 1993 World Bank analysis concluded that most regions of the world could greatly benefit by implementing a limited package of five cost-effective public-health elements. This package could reduce 8% of the burden of disease in low-income countries for $4 per capita and could reduce 4% of the burden in middle-income countries for $7 per capita. The five elements are:

— an extended programme on immunisation;

— school health programmes to treat worm infections and micronutrient deficiencies and to provide health education;

— programmes to increase public knowledge about family planning and nutrition, self-care or indications for seeking care, and vector control and disease surveillance activities;

— programmes to reduce the consumption of tobacco, alcohol, and other drugs;

— AIDS-prevention programmes with a strong component on other sexually transmitted diseases.

The WHO Expert Committee on Comprehensive School Health Education and Promotion commented on this basic package that '[al]though school health programmes are explicitly mentioned in only one of the above elements, for a large portion of the world's population, schools could efficiently provide all five elements of the recommended package'.

The Partnership for Child Development, UNICEF, the World Bank, and other agencies have used this framework to guide programme development in countries around the world. In the state of São Paulo, Brazil, a World Bank loan is helping to provide a broad range of school-based services including feeding programmes, health and nutrition screening of schoolchildren, nutrition and health education in the school curriculum, and school-based programmes for iron and vitamin A supplementation. A more limited package of services with low-cost, easy to implement interventions is applied in Guinea, where almost no prior nutrition and health programmes for school-age children existed. The elements of a school-based health package in Guinea initially include a deworming programme and iron and iodine supplementation, accompanied by education in health and hygiene.

Carefully monitored school-based health and nutrition programmes implemented by the Partnership for Child Development in Ghana, the United Republic of Tanzania, India, and Indonesia have now shown that the education sector is capable of delivering a simple health package (health education, anthelmintics, and micronutrients) to large numbers of schoolchildren (50,000 to 3 million) without the creation of specific infrastructures. These experiences suggest that the school system can contribute to health delivery as long as the package is simple, demands little school time, and is perceived as being appropriate to local needs.

The framework of the child's active learning capacity

In the early 1990s, in support of the mission to achieve Education for All, Beryl Levinger of EDC wrote for USAID and UNDP about the need to concentrate on improving a child's active learning capacity' (ALC). Consistent with theories in education and the social sciences, she defined ALC as 'the child's ability to interact with and take optimal advantage of the full complement of resources offered by any formal or informal learning environment'. The importance of this definition lies in its belief that to maximise learning, a child must be psychologically, emotionally, and physically well, able to concentrate on and participate actively in the learning process, able to pay attention and concentrate on tasks, and missing only a few days of school for illness or other reasons. The ALC framework focuses on improving the quality of life of the child as one of the most important factors in achieving the goals of Education for All.

This framework includes three primary variables: health and nutrition status, hunger level, and psychosocial support. Health and nutrition status refers to both current and prior physical or mental conditions, such as height for age, sensory abilities, nutritional status, and helminthic infections that influence a child's ability to take optimal advantage of learning resources and opportunities. Temporary hunger, especially if a child is malnourished, contributes to a child's distractibility, inattentiveness to environmental stimuli, and adaptive behaviours of passivity and inactivity, all of which impinge on the development of a child's ALC. Psychosocial support encompasses the degree to which parents, caretakers, community leaders, and other significant adults, community institutions, as well as values and norms encourage a child's independence and inquisitiveness and support expectations that favour overall learning as well as formal schooling.

Three variables are considered secondary in determining active learning capacity: prior learning experience, a child's learning receptiveness, and a child's aptitude for learning. Prior learning experience refers to a child's exposure to formal and informal situations conducive to acquiring new knowledge and skills, such as pre-school programmes. Learning receptiveness refers to a child's motivation and attention, which are influenced by health status and hunger level, as well as by the quality of the child/caretaker relationship. Aptitude relates to the time a child needs to learn a particular task, attend to stimuli, and concentrate.

The ALC framework represents a dynamic portrayal of the complex interplay among the determinants of educational outcomes, capturing the high degree of influence that health, nutrition, sensory impairment, and temporary hunger exert on the quality of the child and hence on the child's learning outcomes.

This framework was used widely by the South African Active Learning Network, a group of NGOs, to develop materials, protocols, and broker links between the health and education sectors. Among the entities that participated were CIDA, WHO, UNICEF, the World Bank, and USAID. Many of the Network's activities were designed to promote the ALC model or to further its application.

Importance of frameworks in collaboration

Some of the most important lessons learned in recent years are the need for multisectoral collaboration and co-operation in order to move towards the health and educational goals of Education for All. 'Indicators of a favorable policy setting include a demonstrated ability to secure interministerial cooperation; a co-ordinated, intersectoral approach to human development; a history of support for community-based health and education programs; and a commitment at the highest political levels to programs that address questions of equity as well as growth'.

For example, during the past decade, the World Bank co-ordinated information to enhance the quality of school health and nutrition programmes through its International School Health Initiative. Its experiences of good practice suggest that schoolbased health and nutrition programmes should be simple and locally relevant. The following items have been suggested to contribute to such programmes: life skills training, health services, school snacks fortified with micronutrients, an exemplary school environment, equitable school health policies, and strategies beyond the school. A shared framework and strategy for action often form the foundation of successful collaboration. Even when there is no one unifying framework, collaboration is more likely when the participants at least understand and respect one another's language, methods, and frameworks. In either case, the partners can identify their unique strengths in the context of a framework and channel their specific contributions to move forward a shared agenda.

As the 1990s drew to a close, some of the major leaders and change agents at the world level came together to discuss how they might build on the frameworks since Jomtien and collaborate on a common framework for school health, such as FRESH. Such collaboration may allow partners to harness more effectively their considerable human and financial resources in order to address the health needs of a greater number of children and adolescents in schools around the world.

The FRESH Framework

A framework proposed jointly by WHO, UNICEF, UNESCO, and the World Bank suggests that there is a core group of costeffective components that could form the basis for intensified and joint action. These agencies are now developing a partnership for Focusing Resources on Effective School Health (FRESH), launched at the Education for All Conference in Senegal in April 2000.

Each component of the framework stresses that a young person's health is one of the many important factors that must be adequately addressed to achieve any country's educational goals. As Bundy comments, 'Good health and good education are not ends in themselves, but rather [the] means which provide individuals with the chance to lead productive and satisfying lives. School health is an investment in a country's future and in the capacity of its people to thrive economically and as a society'.

Building on the frameworks developed in the past decade, this shared view serves as a basis for an effective school health and nutrition programme. Its four components are intended to be made available together in all schools.

— *Health-related policies in schools.* Health policies in schools, including policies for skills-based health education and the provision of some health services, can help promote the overall health, hygiene, and nutrition of children. Good health policies should also ensure a safe and secure physical environment and a positive psychosocial environment and should address issues such as the abuse of students, sexual harassment, school violence, and bullying. By guaranteeing the continued education of pregnant schoolgirls and young mothers, school health policies will help promote inclusion and equity in the school environment. Policies that help to prevent and reduce harassment by other students, and even by teachers, also combat the reasons why girls withdraw or are withdrawn from schools. Policies regarding the health practices of teachers and students can reinforce health education by requiring that teachers do not smoke at school and thus act as positive role models for their students. The process of developing and agreeing on policies draws attention to these issues. The policies are best developed by involving many levels, including the national level, and teachers, children, and parents at the school level.

— *Safe water and sanitation facilities.* It is a realistic goal in most countries to ensure that all schools have access to clean water and sanitation. Without clean water and adequate sanitation, hygiene education is meaningless. The school environment may even damage the health and nutritional status of its children if it increases their exposure to hazards such as infectious diseases carried by the water supply. By providing clean water and sanitation, schools can reinforce the health and hygiene messages and act as an example to both students and the wider community. This in turn can lead to a demand from the community for similar facilities. Sound construction policies will help ensure that facilities address issues such as gender access and privacy. Separate facilities for girls, particularly adolescents, are important in reducing drop-out at menstruation and even before. Sound maintenance policies will help ensure the continuing safe use of these facilities.

— *Skills-based health education.* This approach to health, hygiene, and nutrition education focuses on the development of knowledge, attitudes, values, and life skills needed to make and act on the most appropriate and positive decisions concerning health. Health in this context extends beyond the physical to include psychosocial and environmental health issues. The development of attitudes towards gender equity and respect between girls and boys and the development of specific skills, such as dealing with peer pressure, are central to both an effective skills-based health education and positive psychosocial environments. With these skills, individuals are more likely to adopt and sustain a healthy lifestyle during their schooling and for the rest of their lives.

— *School-based health and nutrition services.* Schools can effectively deliver some health and nutrition services as long as the services are simple, safe, and familiar and address problems that are prevalent and recognised as important in the community. If these criteria are met, then the community sees the teacher and school more positively, and teachers see themselves as playing important roles. For example, micronutrient deficiencies and worm infections may be effectively dealt with by infrequent (half-yearly or annual) oral treatment; changing the timing of meals or providing a snack to address short-term hunger

5

Comprehensive Health Education

By themselves, schools cannot and should not be expected to solve serious health and social problems. Families, health care workers, the media, religious organisations, community organisations that serve youth, and young people themselves must also be systematically involved. However, schools could provide a critical facility in which many agencies might work together to protect and promote the health and well-being of young people.

School health programming is most effective when a coordinated approach is planned and implemented. School health education that is not reinforced and supported by other health-promoting actions and aspects of the school environment may increase students' knowledge of health issues, but is unlikely to result in the adoption of health-promoting attitudes and the development and consistent practice of health skills. Because health behaviour, and not merely health knowledge, is the ultimate goal of health education, comprehensive school health education must be implemented within the broader context of a coordinated school health programme. The following are working descriptions of the eight components which should be addressed in a coordinated school health programme.

during the school day - an important constraint on learning - can contribute to school performance; and providing spectacles will allow some children to participate in class fully for the first time.

Within this framework, these four components are intended to be supported by effective partnerships between teachers and health workers, effective community partnerships, and pupil awareness and participation (WHO, UNESCO, UNICEF, World Bank).

1. *Health Education:* A planned, sequential, curriculum, beginning in year one of primary school and continuing through the final year of secondary school, that addresses the physical, mental, emotional and social dimensions of health. The curriculum is designed to motivate and assist students to maintain and improve their health, prevent disease, and reduce health-related risk behaviours. It allows students to develop and demonstrate increasingly sophisticated health-related knowledge, attitudes, skills, and practices. The comprehensive health education curriculum includes a variety of topics such as personal health, family health, community health, consumer health, environmental health, sexuality education, mental and emotional health, injury prevention and safety, nutrition, prevention and control of disease, and substance use and abuse. Qualified, trained teachers provide health education.

2. *Physical Education:* A planned, sequential K-12 curriculum that provides cognitive content and learning experiences in a variety of activity areas such as basic movement skills; physical fitness; rhythms and dance; games; team, dual, and individual sports; tumbling and gymnastics; and aquatics. Quality physical education should promote, through a variety of planned physical activities, each student's optimum physical, mental, emotional, and social development, and should promote activities and sports that all students enjoy and can pursue throughout their lives. Qualified, trained teachers teach physical activity.

3. *Health Services:* Services provided for students to appraise, protect, and promote health. These services are designed to ensure access or referral to primary health care services or both, foster appropriate use of

primary health care services, prevent and control communicable disease and other health problems, provide emergency care for illness or injury, promote and provide optimum sanitary conditions for a safe school facility and school environment, and provide educational and counselling opportunities for promoting and maintaining individual, family, and community health. Qualified professionals such as physicians, nurses, dentists, health educators, and other allied health personnel provide these services.

4. *Nutrition Services:* Access to a variety of nutritious and appealing meals that accommodate the health and nutrition needs of all students. School nutrition programs reflect national dietary guidelines and other criteria to achieve nutrition integrity. The school nutrition services offer students a learning laboratory for classroom nutrition and health education, and serve as a resource for linkages with nutrition-related community services. Qualified child nutrition professionals provide these services.

5. *Health Promotion for Staff:* Opportunities for school staff to improve their health status through activities such as health assessments, health education and health-related fitness activities. These opportunities encourage school staff to pursue a healthy lifestyle that contributes to their improved health status improved morale, and a greater personal commitment to the school's overall coordinated health program. This personal commitment often transfers into greater commitment to the health of students and creates positive role modelling. Health promotion activities have improved productivity, decreased absenteeism, and reduced health insurance costs.

6. *Counselling and Psychological Services:* Services provided to improve students' mental, emotional,

and social health. These services include individual and group assessments, interventions, and referrals. Organisational assessment and consultation skills of counsellors and psychologists contribute not only to the health of students but also to the health of the school environment. Professionals such as certified school counsellors, psychologists, and social workers provide these services.

7. *Healthy School Environment:* The physical and aesthetic surroundings and the psychosocial climate and culture of the school. Factors that influence the physical environment include the school building and the area surrounding it, any biological or chemical agents that are detrimental to health, and physical conditions such as temperature, noise, and lighting. The psychological environment includes the physical, emotional, and social conditions that affect the well-being of students and staff.
8. *Parent/Community Involvement:* An integrated school, parent, and community approach for enhancing the health and well-being of students. School health advisory councils, coalitions, and broadly based constituencies for school health can build support for school health program efforts. Schools actively solicit parent involvement and engage community resources and services to respond more effectively to the health-related needs of students.

Elements of a Comprehensive Health Education Programme

The following are key elements of comprehensive health education, which itself is part of an overall coordinated school health program:

1. A documented, planned, and sequential program of health instruction for students from the first grade of

primary school through the last grade of secondary school.

2. A curriculum that addresses and integrates education about a range of categorical health problems and issues at developmentally appropriate ages.
3. Activities that help young people develop the skills they need to avoid: tobacco use; dietary patterns that contribute to disease; sedentary lifestyle; sexual behaviours that result in HIV infection, other STDs and unintended pregnancy; alcohol and other drug use; and behaviours that result in unintentional and intentional injuries.
4. Instruction provided for a prescribed amount of time at each grade level.
5. Management and coordination by an education professional trained to implement the programme.
6. Instruction from teachers who are trained to teach the subject.
7. Involvement of parents, health professionals, and other concerned community members.
8. Periodic evaluation, updating, and improvement.

   related needs of students.

Understanding Physical Education

Physical Benefits

Physical education is unique to the school curriculum as the only program that provides students with opportunities to learn motor skills, develop fitness and gain understanding about physical activity. Physical benefits gained from physical activity include: disease prevention, safety and injury avoidance, decreased morbidity and premature mortality, and increased mental health. The physical education program is the place where students learn about all of the benefits gained from being physically active as well as the skills and knowledge to incorporate safe, satisfying physical activity into their lives.

Elementary

In the elementary grades, the physical education program emphasizes the development of fundamental locomotor, non-locomotor, and manipulative skills through the main content areas of educational games, dance, and gymnastics. The movement framework, (i.e., body, space, effort, and relationship) is also a part of the core content and is the basis for developing, expanding, and refining children's range of motor skills and awareness. Quality instruction by physical education professionals is critical if children are to develop fundamental motor patterns (e.g. jump, throw, skip, hop, catch, and kick). The motor skill foundations established during the elementary grades may enhance children's social, cognitive and physical development and increase the likelihood of continued interest and participation in physical activity. Fitness at elementary grades is supported by a rich experience in many basic movement forms.

Middle School

The middle school student is ready to experience a wide variety of applications of fundamental movements, including traditional sports, adventure activities (e.g., rock climbing, ropes, kayak, skiing), and lifetime or leisure-oriented activities (e.g., roller-blading, biking, dance). It is during this period when students are capable of refining, combining and applying a variety of sport-related and lifetime skills. Students may explore after-school opportunities for specialised or/and competitive physical activity programs.

Rapid growth during the pre-adolescent years may affect students' interests, choices, and activity patterns. Therefore physical education programs offer a variety of activities to meet and expand student interests. Fitness development becomes more systematic. Students develop specific fitness components, set goals and assess personal fitness levels.

High School

High school students become increasingly more independent as their daily lives become more complex and diversified. High school students begin to make decisions and choices in taking increased responsibility for themselves. Quality high school physical education programs provide students conceptual and practical understanding of: 1) health-related physical fitness, and 2) how to maintain a health-related level of physical fitness. Physical education plays a vital part in helping high school students maintain and refine the skills and knowledge needed to select physical activities to use throughout their lives.

Cognitive Benefits

Children learn through a variety of modalities (e.g., visual, auditory, tactile, physical). Teaching academic concepts through the physical modality may nurture children's kinesthetic intelligence.

Academic constructs have greater meaning for children when they are taught across the three realms of learning, including the cognitive, affective and psychomotor domains. Greater depth and relevance can be achieved when the subject matter constructs are related to each domain of learning. Research has demonstrated that children engaged in daily physical education show superior motor fitness, academic performance, and attitude towards school versus their counterparts who did not participate in daily physical education. Physical education learning experiences also offer a unique opportunity for problem solving, self-expression, socialisation, and conflict resolution.

Elementary

Research suggests that young children learn through active engagement with the "stuff" of their world. Children in elementary school acquire knowledge through physical exploration of their environment. Physical education may provide children with learning experiences essential to the formation of mental schemes (i.e., mental patterns or systems that describe the ways people think about the world; building blocks of thinking). Children form more effective schemes by physically interacting with their environment. Quality physical education programs facilitate exploration of movement in various contexts that enhance acquisition of knowledge.

Middle School

Middle school students are intensely curious, prefer active to passive learning, and definitely favor interaction with peers during learning activities. The early adolescent exhibits a strong willingness to learn things they consider useful. They enjoy using skills to solve real life problems. Quality physical education programs provide a medium through which middle school students can refine and expand upon their physical repertoire of skills. It has been shown that students miss fewer days of school because of illness and exhibit greater academic achievement because of the physical vitality gained in physical education.

High School

During the high school years students should be given

more in-depth learning opportunities so they can understand the mechanical, physiological and socialpsychological aspects of physical activity. High school students' growing ability to compare and contrast, analyse, and synthesize information enables them to apply movement principles in new and meaningful ways. Students can more fully understand the role of physical activity in preventive health and analyse the pros and cons of various types of physical activity in lifelong health.

Affective Benefits

Physical competence builds self-esteem. Quality physical education programs enhance the development of both competence and confidence in performing motor skills. Attitudes, habits, and perceptions are critical prerequisites for persistent participation in physical activity. Appropriate levels of health-related fitness enhance feelings of well being and efficacy.

Elementary

Quality physical education programs can contribute to the development of selfesteem among children. Children who are more active may have greater social success and positive relations with peers. Children need many opportunities to experience personal feelings of success and achievement in physical activity settings. Explorations of various movement capabilities contribute to feelings of joy and accomplishment.

Middle School

Quality middle school physical education programs provide students unique opportunities for demonstrating leadership, socialisation, and goal setting skills. Involvement in physical activity has shown a consistent relationship with mood, self-esteem, and other indices of psychological well-being in early adolescence. Student preferences become more specialised at this age and the preference influences students' motivation to continue in physical activities.

A youngster's feelings of perceived competence also affects future participation and selfesteem. Despite the physiological changes that occur at this age, students are generally willing to work cooperatively toward common goals because the desire for peer group acceptance is strong. Risk taking is attractive and students accept the challenge of setting and achieving personal goals. Physical education programs have a unique opportunity to provide learning experiences that enhance middle school students' self-esteem.

High School

During this phase of development, students begin to select activities based more on personal interests. Other factors affecting students' choices of physical activity may be their level of health-related physical fitness, body type, geographical location, and socio-economic group or circle of peers. Physical education programs must continue to enhance students' fitness development and offer an array of activities from which students can select.

Attitudes, habits, and perceptions are critical prerequisites for persistent participation in physical activities. To help students achieve self-realisation through physical activity, the physical education program can guide student choices and help them become self-directed in the selection of activities that are satisfying.

The importance of commitment and dedication in achieving success may be emphasized in physical education. Physical activity habits and preferences are not static, but are continually in a state of flux throughout one's lifetime. High school is a time when students can establish habits and attitudes about the role physical activity will play in their lifetime. This is the time for students to explore their preferences related to physical activity and perhaps specialise based on abilities and interests.

Physical Activity Improves the Quality of Life

Regular physical activity improves functional status and limits disability during the middle and later adult years. Physical activity contributes to quality of life, psychological health, and the ability to meet physical work demands. Physical education can serve as a vehicle for helping students to develop the knowledge, attitudes, motor skills, behavioral skills, and confidence needed to adopt and maintain physically active lifestyles.

The outcomes of a quality physical education program include the development of students' physical competence, health-related fitness, self-esteem, and overall enjoyment of physical activity. These outcomes enable students to make informed decisions and choices about leading a physically active lifestyle.

In early years children derive pleasure from movement sensations and experience challenge and joy as they sense a growing competence in their movement ability. Evidence suggests that the level of participation, the degree of skill, and the number of activities mastered as a child directly influences the extent to which children will continue to participate in physical activity as an adult. In early adolescence participation in physical activity provides important opportunities for challenge, social interaction, group membership, as well as opportunities for continued personal growth in physical skill.

Participation for high school students continues to provide enjoyment and challenge as young people express preferences for activities that meet their specific interests. A comprehensive, well-implemented physical education program is an essential component to the total education of students. Physical education prepares students to maintain healthy, active lifestyles and engage in enjoyable, meaningful leisure-time pursuits.

School Health Policy Development

Policies provide an essential framework for achieving the goals and objectives of a school's overall school health programme. They should cover all issues identified through a community needs assessment as having an impact on the health of students and school staff. If a good mix of individuals works together to determine the content of policies, including school personnel, students, parents, community leaders and experts, the process itself helps to build consensus and support for the school's health programme activities. Use the information that follows to assess the adequacy of existing policies at your school, and to decide how those policies should be improved.

Determining what will be included in school health policies

Policies may cover any or all of the following issues:

- Rights, discrimination and gender issues, e.g.:
  - discrimination related to differences in religion, caste or ethnic origin
  - sexual harassment and abuse
  - continued education for pregnant and parenting students
  - continued employment of staff and education of students infected or affected by HIV or AIDS
- Inclusive practices for students with special needs, e.g.:

  - special education services
  - education and services (such as speech, occupational and physical therapy, counselling, etc.) for students with disabilities
  - continuing education for pregnant or parenting teens
- Environmental concerns, e.g.:
  - water and sanitation facilities
  - food service conditions
  - the safety of school buildings and grounds
  - elimination of toxins (asbestos, lead, etc.)
  - accessibility for students with disabilities
- Health education programmes, e.g.:
  - requirements for classes
  - teacher training and credentialing
  - curricula content
- School-wide/community-wide efforts to address significant health problems, e.g.:
  - to decrease drug, alcohol and tobacco use
  - to increase physical activity
  - to decrease the spread of HIV and other sexually transmitted infections and reduce AIDS-related discrimination
  - unintended injuries and violence
- School feeding programmes
- Health services, e.g.:
  - immunisation requirements
  - health screening
  - health records

- — exclusion for and prevention of communicable disease
- — medical treatment for helminth infections, nutritional deficiencies and other illnesses
- — HIV infection
- — credentials for health service providers

— Emergency•procedures and responsibilities

Coordinated school health programmes most often include the following eight components:

1. Health education
2. Physical education
3. School health services
4. Nutrition services
5. Healthy school environment
6. Counselling, psychological, and social services
7. Health promotion for staff
8. Parent and community involvement.

Evidence-based Physical Activity Promotion

The importance of physical activity for health, or healthenhancing physical activity (HEPA), has been well established. Early important syntheses were "Moving On", by the UK Health Education Authority, and the US Surgeon General's Report on Physical Activity and Health, but extensive research has been conducted since that has contributed to the body of knowledge. Physical inactivity has been identified as a leading risk factor in recent "world health reports" of the World Health Organisation.

While a standardised method for the population assessment of HEPA has only recently been introduced, the estimates available so far emphasise the public health relevance of the issue: 17% of the adult global population are estimated to be physically inactive, and another 41% are only insufficiently active for health benefits. For the three European WHO subregions for which the "world health report" provides estimates, the proportion of inactive individuals ranges between 16% and 24%. WHO also estimates that, each year, physical inactivity causes 1.9 million premature deaths globally and some 600,000 in the European Region alone.

Sports-for-all promotion has a long history in many countries, but only a few examples of long-term integrated physical activity promotion strategies were in place until about 10 years ago, notably those in Finland and Canada. Since then, large national programs have been launched, first in England and the Netherlands, but later also in other countries. During the same period, there has been a growth in research into the health effects of physical activity, and work has also begun to focus on assessing the effectiveness of interventions.

Role of International Structures and Contacts

Early concepts already have defined that HEPA can take place in leisure time, at work or in domestic duties; more recent models also include physical activity for transport as a fourth domain. International organisations have been essential in promoting the concept of regular physical activity and the recommendation of at least half an hour of moderate-intensity activities a day. WHO has played an important role, with the WHO Global Initiative for Active Living, the Move for Health Day and, most recently, its Global Strategy on Diet, Physical Activity and Health, along with other health organisations such as the World Heart Federation and the International Diabetes Federation. From 1996 until 2001, the first European Network for the Promotion of Health-Enhancing Physical

Activity existed as a programme funded by the European Union (EU) and was instrumental in facilitating exchange and providing support for the development of integrated national approaches.

The specific products of the network have been influential not only because of their content but also because of the process by which they were developed. For example, the inclusion of "Allez Hop!" in the analyses for the "Guidelines for Health-Enhancing Physical Activity Promotion Programmes" has had a political impact on the national scale in Switzerland and led to further support for the project. The European Network for the Promotion of Health-Enhancing Physical Activity was exclusively funded by the EU DG SANCO programme. Unfortunately, this support was no longer granted after 2001.

International activities in the field of environment and health have recently started to address transport-related physical activity also. The WHO Charter on Transport, Environment and Health, adopted by the Third Ministerial Conference on Environment and Health, set a policy framework that acknowledges the role of transportrelated physical activity in the attainment of better health. The document "Promotion of Transport Walking and Cycling in Europe: Strategy Directions" of the first European Network has provided a valuable basis for further development, for example in the "Transnational Project Transport-Related Health Effects with a Particular Focus On Children".

The number of congresses and publications covering physical activity and health has increased considerably over the last few years, and the possibilities for exchange about the scientific aspects of health effects of physical activity, about methodological issues and about the effectiveness of interventions have improved accordingly. However, after the end of the first European Network, there was no forum for regular exchange of information, nor was there an international platform supporting the development of national strategies for physical activity promotion. The nongovernmental organisation Agita Mundo provides these functions on the global level, but both practicality and cultural similarities favour a European structure. This is even more important now that many European countries are following the call of WHO's Global Strategy to develop and implement their national strategies. At the same time, a growing wealth of experience and evidence exists but is often not available to health promotion practitioners in the field or in national administrations. Only a small proportion of the evidence exists in the form of publications in scientific journals, and many documents are in the form of reports that are often only available in local languages. Some considerations for physical activity policy development exist, but more work has to be done to provide concepts that can be applied in practice.

HEPA Europe

In this situation, the idea for a new European Physical Activity Promotion Network was developed during an international Physical Activity Expert Meeting in Magglingen, Switzerland, in June 2004. The Swiss Federal Offices of Sports and Public Health provided financial support for the first phase of the network, and the WHO European Centre for Environment and Health in Rome is working closely with it. An intermediate steering committee started working, and the founding meeting of HEPA Europe, the new European Network for the Promotion of Health-Enhancing Physical Activity, took place at the Gerlev Physical Education and Sports Academy in Denmark in May of 2005. A steering committee was established, and the cornerstones of the network were defined.

HEPA Europe will contribute to the development of the evidence base on both the health effects of physical activity and on the effectiveness of approaches to physical activity promotion. The network will work to make this evidence easily available and provide specific expertise to other partners in order to contribute to the development and implementation of national policies and strategies for HEPA in Europe. It wants to develop, support and disseminate effective strategies, programmes, approaches and other examples of good practice. HEPA Europe supports and facilitates the development of multisectoral approaches to physical activity promotion, and the members of the network serve as experts to a whole range of organisations and projects, including WHO Headquarters, WHO Europe's 2006 Ministerial Conference on Counteracting Obesity, the Pan-European Programme on Transport, Environment and Health and the EU Platform on Diet, Physical Activity and Health.

The role of physical activity in the prevention of overweight and obesity is a very important one, and the WHO Global Strategy on Diet, Physical Activity and Health states: "Diet and physical activity influence health both together and separately. Although the effects of diet and physical activity on health often interact, particularly in relation to obesity, there are additional health benefits to be gained from physical activity that are independent of nutrition and diet, and there are significant nutritional risks that are unrelated to obesity. Physical activity is a fundamental means of improving the physical and mental health of individuals." From the public health perspective, the main disease burden comes from cardiovascular diseases, overweight and obesity and other metabolic diseases such as type 2 diabetes, several types of cancer and osteoporosis. Because physical activity can substantially reduce the risk of all these diseases, HEPA Europe does not limit its scope to any single health effect of physical activity promotion.

Collaboration with the European Union and global partnerships

Physical activity is addressed, together with nutrition, in the Community Public Health Programme, 2003-2008, of the EU. The recent launch of the EU Platform on Diet, Physical Activity and Health by the Directorate General for Health and Consumer Affairs DG SANCO is part of the overall strategy on nutrition and physical activity being developed by the EU Commission and follows discussions with various stakeholders about ways to address the obesity epidemic in Europe. Within the programme, the commission finances projects aimed at collecting data on obesity, nutrition and physical activity, as well as projects aimed at promoting healthy diets and physical activity.

A very close relationship covering virtually all projects of HEPA Europe has been established with one of these projects, the "European Network on Public Health, Nutrition and Physical Activity" and its task forces on Physical Activity and Monitoring. In addition, HEPA Europe is collaborating with the Lifestyle Working Party Secretariat, which organised the meeting on Monitoring of Physical Activity in September 2005 in Cyprus. More possibilities for joint projects are being actively explored. On the global level, HEPA Europe has joined Agita Mundo and is also cooperating with the Global Alliance on Physical Activity (GAPA), which is currently emerging from a cooperative agreement of the International Union for Health Promotion and Education (IUHPE) with the US Centers for Disease Control and Prevention (US CDC). This alliance is coordinated from the School of Sport & Exercise Sciences at Loughborough University, UK; it is global in scope and wants to coordinate and provide strategic orientation to the activities and actions developed by nongovernmental organisations (NGOs) as well as civil society.

Current Projects and Activities

The direct use for the practice of physical activity promotion and intersectoral approaches are priorities of HEPA Europe. The first project of the network is a collection of case studies of collaboration between the physical activity promotion sector and the transport sector, which is carried out by the University of Basel, Switzerland and funded by the Swiss Federal Offices of Sports and Public Health. The second project is a critical review paper of health effects related to physical activity in cost-benefit and cost-effectiveness analyses of investments in transport infrastructures and policies. The work is carried out at the Karolinska Institute in Stockholm, Sweden, and funded through resources made available to the WHO European Centre for Environment and Health by the Swedish Government.

A number of further projects have been defined in the work programme 2005-2006. Interested organisations have the opportunity to join HEPA Europe, to contribute their knowledge and expertise, to benefit from experiences that have already been made and to participate in the process of this new pan-European platform at the interface between science and policymaking. Better health through physical activity is the vision of the European Network for the Promotion of Health-Enhancing Physical Activity. The public health importance of healthy lifestyles and conditions favourable to physical activity is only beginning to emerge, and together with its partners, HEPA Europe wants to provide the framework and the substance to address these issues.

Effective School Health

"Education for All" means ensuring that all children have access to basic education of good quality. This implies creating an environment in schools and in basic education programmes in which children are both able and enabled to learn. Such an environment must be inclusive of children, effective with children, friendly and welcoming to children, healthy and protective for children and gender sensitive. The development of such child-friendly learning environments is an essential part of the overall efforts by countries around the world to increase access to, and improve the quality of, their schools.

Poor health and malnutrition are important underlying factors for low school enrollment, absenteeism, poor classroom performance, and early school dropout, as reflected in the World Declaration on Education for All. Programmes to achieve good health, hygiene and nutrition at school age are therefore essential to the promotion of basic education for all children.

Good health and nutrition are not only essential inputs but also important outcomes of basic education of good quality. First, children must be healthy and well-nourished in order to fully participate in education and gain its maximum benefits. Early childhood care programmes and primary schools which improve children's health and nutrition can enhance the learning and educational outcomes of school children. Second, education of good quality can lead to better health and nutrition outcomes for children, especially girls, and thus for the next generation of children as well. In addition, a healthy, safe and secure school environment can help protect children from health hazards, abuse and exclusion.

Ensuring that children are healthy and able to learn is an essential component of an effective education system. This is especially relevant to efforts to achieve education for all in the most deprived areas. Increased enrollment and reduced absenteeism and drop-out bring more of the poorest and most disadvantaged children to school, many of whom are girls. It is these children who are often the least healthy and most malnourished, who have the most to gain educationally from improved health. Effective school health programmes that are developed as part of community partnerships provide one of the most cost-effective ways to reach adolescents and the broader community and are a sustainable means of promoting healthy practices.

Improving the health and learning of school children through school-based health and nutrition programmes is not a new concept. Many countries have school health programmes, and many agencies and non-government organisations (NGO's) have decades of experience. These common experiences suggest an opportunity for concerted action by a partnership of agencies and NGO's to broaden the scope of school health programmes and make them more effective. Effective school health programmes will contribute to the development of child-friendly schools and thus to the promotion of education for all.

This interagency initiative has identified a core group of activities, each already recommended by the participating agencies, that captures the best practices from programme experiences. Focusing initially on these activities will allow concerted action by the participating agencies, and will ensure consistent advice to country programmes and projects. Because of the focused and collaborative nature of this approach, it will increase the number of countries able to implement school health components of childfriendly school reforms, and help ensure that these programmes go to scale. The focused actions are seen as a starting point to which other interventions may be added as appropriate.

The actions also contribute to existing agency initiatives. They are an essential component of the "health promoting schools" initiative of WHO and of global efforts by UNICEF, UNESCO and the World Bank to make schools effective as well as healthy, hygienic and safe. Overall, the inter-agency action is perceived as Focusing Resources on Effective School Health and giving a FRESH Start to improving the quality and equity of education.

Focusing Resources on the School-Age Child

A child's ability to attain her or his full potential is directly related to the synergistic effect of good health, good nutrition and appropriate education. Good health and good education are not only ends in themselves, but also means which provide individuals with the chance to lead productive and satisfying lives. School health is an investment in a country's future and in the capacity of its people to thrive economically and as a society.

An effective school health, hygiene and nutrition programme offers many benefits:

Responds to a new need

The success of child survival programmes and the greater efforts by many governments and communities to expand basic education coverage have resulted both in a greater number of school-age children and in a greater proportion of these children attending school. In many countries, targeted education programmes have ensured that many of these new entrants are girls for whom good health is especially important. Thus, the school is now a key setting where the health and education sectors can jointly take action to improve and sustain the health, nutrition and education of children previously beyond reach.

Increases the efficacy of other investments in child development

School health programmes are the essential sequel and complement to early childhood care and development programmes. Increasing numbers of countries have programmes that ensure that a child enters a school fit, well and ready to learn. But the school-age child continues to be at risk of ill health throughout the years of schooling. Good health at school age is essential if children are to sustain the advantages of a healthy early childhood and take full advantage of what may be their only opportunity for formal learning. Furthermore, school health programmes can help ensure that the children who enter school without benefit of early development programmes receive the attention they may need to take full advantage of their educational opportunity.

Ensures better educational outcomes

Although school children have a lower mortality rate than infants, they do suffer from highly prevalent conditions that can adversely affect their development. Micronutrient deficiencies, common parasitic infections, poor vision and hearing, and disability can have a detrimental effect on school enrolment and attendance, and on cognition and educational achievement. In older children, avoidance of risky behaviours can reduce dropping out due, for example, to early pregnancy. Ensuring good health at schoolage can boost school enrolment and attendance, reduce the need for repetition and increase educational attainment, while good health practices can promote reproductive health and help limit the spread of HIV/AIDS.

Achieves greater social equity

As a result of universal basic education strategies, some of the most disadvantaged children - girls, the rural poor, children with disabilities - are for the first time having access to school. But their ability to attend school and to learn whilst there is compromised by poor health. These are the children who will benefit most from health interventions, since they are likely to show the greatest improvements in attendance and learning achievement. School health programmes can thus help modify the effects of socioeconomic and gender-related inequities.

Is a highly cost effective strategy

School health programmes help link the resources of the health, education, nutrition, and sanitation sectors in an infrastructure - the school - that is already in place, is pervasive and is sustained. While the school system is rarely universal, its coverage is often superior to health systems and it may have an extensive skilled workforce that already works closely with the community. The accessibility of school health programmes to a large proportion of each nation's population, staff as well as students, contributes to the low cost of programmes. The high effectiveness of these programmes is a consequence of the synergy between the health benefit and the educational benefit. The effectiveness is measurable in terms not only of improved health and nutrition, but also of improved educational outcomes, reduced wastage, less repetition and generally enhanced returns on educational investments.

Basic Framework for an Effective School Health and Nutrition Programme

The framework described here is the starting point for developing an effective school health component in broader efforts to achieve more effective, child-friendly schools. Much more could be done, but if all schools implement these four interventions there would be a significant immediate benefit, and a basis for future expansion. In particular, the aim is to focus on interventions that are feasible to implement even in the most resource-poor schools and in hard-to-reach rural areas as well as in accessible urban areas, and that promote learning through improved health and nutrition. These are actions known to be effective, and actively endorsed by all the supporting agencies: this is a framework from which individual countries will develop their own strategy to match local needs. Core framework for action: four components that should be made available together, in all schools.

(i) Health-related school policies

Health policies in schools, including skills-based health education and the provision of some health services, can help promote the overall health, hygiene and nutrition of children. But good health policies should go beyond this to ensure a safe and secure physical environment and a positive psycho-social environment, and should address issues such as abuse of students, sexual harassment, school violence, coporal punishment and bullying. By guaranteeing the further education of pregnant schoolgirls and young mothers, school health policies will help promote inclusion and equity in the school environment. Policies that help to prevent and reduce harassment by other students and even by teachers, also help to fight against reasons that girls withdraw or are withdrawn from schools. Policies regarding the health-related practices of teachers and students can reinforce health education: teachers can act as positive role models for their students, for example, by not smoking in school. The process of developing and agreeing upon policies draws attention to these issues. The policies are best developed by involving many levels, including the national level, and teachers, children, and parents at the school level.

(ii) Provision of safe water and sanitation -the essential first steps towards a healthy learning environment.

The school environment may damage the health and nutritional status of school children, particularly if it increases their exposure to hazards such as infectious disease carried by the water supply. Hygiene education is meaningless without clean water and adequate sanitation facilities. It is a realistic goal in most countries to ensure that all schools have access to clean water and sanitation. By providing these facilities, schools can reinforce health and hygiene messages, and act as an example to both students and the wider community. This in turn can lead to a demand for similar facilities from the community. Sound construction policies will help ensure that facilities address issues such as gender access and privacy. Separate facilities for girls, particularly adolescent girls, are an important contributing factor to reducing dropout at menses and even before. Sound maintenance policies will help ensure the continuing safe use of these facilities.

(iii) Skills based health education

This approach to health, hygiene and nutrition education focuses upon the development of knowledge, attitudes, values, and life skills needed to make and act on the most appropriate and positive health-related decisions. Health in this context extends beyond physical health to include psycho-social and environmental health issues. Changes in social and behavioural factors have given greater prominence to such health-related issues as HIV/AIDS, early pregnancy, injuries, violence and tobacco and substance abuse. Unhealthy social and behavioural factors not only influence lifestyles, health and nutrition, but also hinder education opportunities for a growing number of school-age children and adolescents. The development of attitudes related to gender equity and respect between girls and boys, of skills such as dealing with peer pressure, is central to effective skills-based health education and positive psycho-social environments. When individuals have such skills, they are more likely to adopt and sustain a healthy lifestyle during schooling and for the rest of their lives.

(iv) School-based health and nutrition services

Schools can effectively deliver some health and nutritional services provided that the services are simple, safe and familiar and address problems that are prevalent and recognised as important within the community. If these criteria are met then the community sees the teacher and school more positively, and teachers perceive themselves as playing important roles. For example, micronutrient deficiencies and worm infections may be effectively dealt with by infrequent (six-monthly or annual) oral treatment; changing the timing of meals, or providing a snack to address short term hunger during school -an important constraint on learning - can contribute to school performance; and providing spectacles will allow some children to fully participate in class for the first time.

Supporting Strategies

Several strategies can support the implementation of the above components of FRESH:

(i) Effective partnerships between teachers and health workers and between the education and health sectors

The success of school health programmes demands an effective partnership between Ministries of Education and Health, and between teachers and health workers. The health sector retains the responsibility for the health of children, but the education sector is responsible for implementing, and often funding, school based programmes. These sectors need to identify respective responsibilities and present coordinated action to improve health and learning outcomes for children.

(ii) Effective community partnerships

Promoting a positive interaction between the school and the community is fundamental to the success and sustainability of any school improvement process. Community partnerships engender a sense of collaboration, commitment and communal ownership. Such partnerships also build public awareness and strengthen demand. Within the school health component of such improvement processes, parental support and cooperation allow education about health to be shared and reinforced at home. The involvement of the broader community (e.g. the private sector, community organisations and women's groups) can enhance and reinforce school health promotion and resources.

(iii) Pupil awareness and participation

Children must be important participants in all aspects of school health programmes, and not simply the beneficiaries. Children who participate in health policy development and implementation; in efforts to create a safer and more sanitary environment; in health promotion aimed at their parents, other children, and community members; and in school health services, learn about health by doing. This is an effective way to help young people acquire the knowledge, attitudes, values and skills needed to adopt healthy lifestyles and to support health and Education for All.

6

Poverty Gender and Health Education

The term violence against women has been used to describe many different acts, ranging from murder and rape to sexual harassment and emotional abuse. Clarity on the terms used is important to properly understand the magnitude and dimensions of the problem and to assess its health consequences.

Gender-based Violence

The UN Declaration on the Elimination of Violence Against Women (Article 1) defines violence against women as:

> Any act of gender-based violence that results in, or is likely to result in, physical, sexual or psychological harm or suffering to women, including threats of such acts, coercion or arbitrary deprivation of liberty, whether occurring in public or private life.

Article 2 of the Declaration further specifies that violence against women should include, but not be limited to:

> Acts of physical, sexual and psychological violence whether they be in the family or the community. The acts of violence specified in this article include: spousal battering, sexual abuse of female children, dowry-related violence, rape including marital rape, traditional practices

harmful to women such as female genital mutilation, non-spousal violence, sexual harassment and intimidation, trafficking in women, forced prostitution, and violence perpetrated or condoned by the state such as rape in war.

Forms of gender-based violence

Violence can be divided into four categories :

— Physical violence

— Sexual violence

— Psychological/emotional violence (including coercive tactics)

— Threat of physical or sexual violence

Physical violence is defined as the intentional use of physical force with the potential to cause death, disability, injury or harm. However, violence takes many forms besides physical assault. Many women and girls experience some form of sexual violence during their lifetime, ranging from sexual harassment in public spaces to abusive sexual contact, coercive sex by an intimate partner, and rape.

While acts of physical and sexual violence may be dramatic events readily acknowledged as unacceptable, psychological or emotional violence is more insidious and pervasive. Psychological or emotional violence is defined as trauma to the victim caused by acts, threats of acts and coercive tactics when there has also been prior physical or sexual violence, or prior threat of physical or sexual violence. In addition to actual acts of violence, any act that communicates the threat of physical and sexual violence is in itself classified as a form of violence.

Gender-based violence through the lifecycle

Violence against girls and women occurs at different points in their lifecycle. Many women experience multiple episodes of violence that may start in the prenatal period and continue through childhood to adulthood and old age. The lifecycle approach to gender-based violence helps one understand the cumulative impact of violence experienced by girls and women, especially in terms of its physical and mental health consequences.

Intimate partner violence or domestic violence

The most common and endemic form of violence experienced by women all over the world is violence by the spouse or intimate partner. This is often referred to as 'domestic violence'.

Intimate partner violence takes many forms, including physical, sexual and psychological violence over a prolonged period of time. Studies on the nature of intimate partner violence and its manifestations find that there is a 'cycle of violence' that becomes difficult to break. In the first phase of this cycle, there is a gradual increase in tension and conflicts between the couple. The woman tries to appease her partner, generating a false sense of being able to control his aggression. The second phase is one of open, 'explosive' aggression, characterised by physical, sexual and psychological abuse. This phase ends when the aggressor stops the abuse temporarily. A period of reconciliation, or the 'honeymoon' phase, follows. The abuser shows remorse and promises to rectify his behaviour. He may be especially loving and kind, which assures the woman that there is a 'good' side to her partner, which she can retain by adopting appropriate behaviour. This third phase makes her feel that it is not necessary to leave the relationship.

The 'cycle of violence' explains why many women stay in abusive relationships. Over time, they begin to adjust to their partner's violent behaviour by modifying their own. They develop a strategy for survival that may include extreme passivity, even defending the aggressor. Violence in the relationship becomes entrenched and the affected women appear to make no moves to change the situation. Over time, the 'aggression' phase may become more frequent and intense, and could even end in death unless the cycle is broken through sustained external interventions to help the woman.

Documenting the incidence of gender-based violence is a difficult and sensitive task fraught with methodological difficulties as well as ethical dilemmas. To begin with, there is a need to define different categories of violence precisely.

A more complex issue relates to recruitment and retention of interviewees. Approaches that do not involve face-to-face interaction, such as telephone interviews and postal surveys, have the benefit of ensuring confidentiality and privacy for the respondent. However, these may not be the best methodologies when studying lower-income groups, and in many developing country settings. Health center-based recruitment may be useful in getting a larger number of respondents but will not be a representative population, making it unsuitable for estimation of incidence and prevalence.

Community-based surveys involving face-to-face interviews are increasingly being used to get information on population prevalence rates of different forms of gender-based violence and especially intimate-partner violence. This poses a number of ethical dilemmas. The major concern in such surveys is the safety of the respondent. Asking women about their experiences of violence may place them at a high risk of being victimised again by the perpetrator. In having to think about and report on the violence they have experienced, women may experience stress and trauma all over again.

The World Health Organisation has formulated ethical and safety recommendations for conducting communitybased surveys on gender-based violence, stressing that nothing is more important than the respondent's safety.

Another difficult methodological issue relates to the reliability of self-reported rates of violence. It is acknowledged that women may be reluctant to report violence, especially intimate partner violence, for reasons such as fear of reprisal or, more often, because they have not defined their experience as 'violence' or 'abuse', even to themselves. The consequence is under-reporting of the prevalence of violence. When studies document lower levels of violence than is actually the case, they may be doing more harm than good because such research may be used to question the importance of gender-based violence as a legitimate area of concern. Questions need to be carefully formulated and sequenced, and interviewers trained meticulously in order to minimise under-reporting as well as to uphold ethical and safety standards when conducting the survey.

Despite these numerous difficulties in documenting the extent and nature of gender-based violence, some progress has been made in recent years. The State of world population report 2000 and the World report on violence and health present information on physical assault by intimate partners and on sexual violence from several countries.

Studies suggest that almost all instances of physical assault by an intimate partner are accompanied by psychological abuse and, in one-third to one-half of cases, by sexual abuse. In a study of 360 women in Nicaragua who had ever had an intimate partner, one-fifth had experienced physical, psychological as well as sexual violence from their partners at some point. The most common sources of information on sexual violence, especially rape and assault by a stranger, are crime statistics. These may be seen to represent only the tip of the iceberg, as only a very small percentage of sexual violence is reported, and sexual violence by an intimate partner may never get reported at all.

Gender and Gender-based Violence

Factors underlying gender-based violence

Gender-based violence is perpetrated on girls and women primarily because of their gender identity. What makes it different from other forms of violence is that gender-based violence is often socially sanctioned.

Gender roles and norms prevalent in society

Gender-based violence emerges in part from a system of gender relations that assumes male superiority, domination and control over women as the normal order of things, a matter of 'culture'. Socially constructed gender roles and norms vest men with greater access to and control over power and resources, and these are usually reinforced by social institutions, such as the family, school, the work place and religious institutions. Male authority and control over resources is often sanctioned by law, as in the case of marriage, divorce, and inheritance laws in many countries.

Multiple expressions of violence such as lower investment in girls' education and health relative to that for boys, forced marriages, feet binding, female genital mutilation and honour killings have for centuries been considered normal and validated by custom. Further, violence and the threat of violence have been used as instruments to 'keep women in their place' and punish women who step 'out of line' or do not adhere to societal norms regarding 'appropriate' female behaviour. Thus, in many societies, failure to cook a meal on time or wash a partner's clothes could provoke violence within the household, while venturing out in the community without a male escort could result in a severe reprimand from members of the neighbourhood and community.

The environment in which men are socialised is seen as an important contributor to gender-based violence. The ideas, images and norms that they grow up with, and glorification of the aggressive "macho" man in television, movies and advertising systematically develop values in boys that define being male as synonymous with being aggressive and controlling women. It is also known from research that men who grow up witnessing abuse of women are more likely to themselves become abusers.

In studies on masculinity and gender violence carried out in four sites in India in 2001-2002, a consistent association was found between men's rigid adherence to gender roles and expectations and their reporting of violent behaviour with their wives. There was a difference between men who reported only physical violence and those who reported sexual violence. The former resorted to physical abuse to ensure that their wives conformed to expected female roles. However, those who engaged in sexual violence were less concerned with gender roles and more concerned about power and control over all aspects of their wives' lives.

Power and control wheel

Power and control over women's lives have been acknowledged as the basis of gender violence by the intimate partner and in society at large. The 'Power and Control' wheel offers a framework for understanding manifestations and mechanisms of power and control in an intimate relationship. These mechanisms include for example, intimidation, cutting off a person's access to cash, restricting her employment opportunities, isolation and emotional abuse. The power and control wheel may be adapted to also understand societal expressions of power and control over women. For example, laws that restrict women's property rights may be seen as the societal equivalent of economic abuse.

While unequal gender relations and men's control over all aspects of women's lives lie at the core of gender-based violence, a number of individual factors are associated with an elevated risk of experiencing such violence. These include, for example, a history of violence in the family, alcohol abuse by men, and personality disorders. However, no single factor can be identified as the principal 'cause' of gender violence. Further, factors underlying gender violence operate at various levels, and not just at the personal level.

The 'ecological model'

The 'ecological' model proposed by Heise consists of four levels of causative factors visualised as four embedded concentric circles (Figure 1). The innermost circle represents the personal history of the woman and man in a relationship. It includes factors such as childhood experiences of witnessing marital violence or themselves having been abused. The second circle represents the immediate context within which violence takes place and may include factors such as male dominance and marital tensions and conflict. The third circle represents the 'ecosystem' factors: the institutions and structures that influence the immediate context. Ecosystem factors include women's autonomy and access to resources and their social support network.

The fourth circle represents the macro context within which the other three circles are imbedded, and consists of factors such as gender roles, acceptance of power hierarchies in general, and acceptance of interpersonal violence.

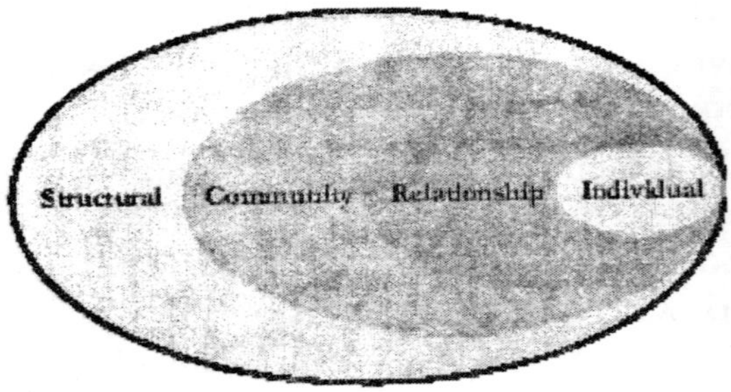

Figure 1. Ecological Framework for Understanding Violence

This framework helps understand variations in the prevalence of violence within a given society and also across time. It helps us understand the complex interaction of factors at various levels which increase the probability of a man being abusive within a given setting in a given relationship at a particular point in time.

Gender-based Violence and Poverty

Poverty as an underlying factor in gender-based violence

Although women from all socioeconomic groups experience gender violence, an increasing number of studies from different parts of the world show that low-income women experience a greater incidence of violence, especially intimate partner violence.

Many of these studies have related to welfare recipients in industrialised countries. For example, a study of a representative sample of women welfare recipients in Massachusetts found that 64 % had experienced violence by a current or former partner and almost 20% had experienced intimate partner violence in the preceding 12 months. In a 1997 study of intimate partner violence and black women's health, low-income black women had much higher rates of severe intimate partner violence as compared to higher-income black women. The reasons for this association are not clearly understood and need further analysis. Factors associated with poverty, such as living in unsafe neighbourhoods and lack of secure housing, may explain the risk of violence outside the home. Within intimate relationships, arguments over money, hopelessness, crowding and the stress of finding a means of living may be factors that precipitate violence.

The Voices of the poor report of the World Bank suggests that, in some settings, gender violence may be increasing in low-income households because of rapidly changing gender roles. There is increasing economic pressure on poor households, with men in many parts of the world having lost their traditional occupations and jobs. Women have been forced to take on or increase their income-earning activities in addition to their domestic tasks. The relative increase in women's economic power, combined with men's unemployment and limited access to resources, has created feelings of humiliation and emasculation among men and a sense of loss of control within their households. Men's frustration and anger at not being able to fulfil their traditional roles as breadwinners often leads to increasing levels of tension and violence.

Gender-based violence as a cause of poverty and economic hardship

Irrespective of their original socioeconomic status, many women experience financial risks or are impoverished as a consequence of gender violence. After experiencing sexual assault or sexual harassment at work or in a public place, they may be unable to continue in their jobs or perform their jobs efficiently and may frequently have to take time-off from work. They may lose opportunities for further training or promotion because of their unwillingness to risk their safety. Young women fleeing situations of sexual abuse in their immediate setting may drop out of school with limited job skills, restricting their future income-earning opportunities.

Men who batter their intimate partners usually control them through restricted access to cash and credit, isolation from others, and sabotage of educational and job training and employment opportunities. Women choosing to walk away from such relationships may have to leave their jobs and their homes. Safety considerations may mean not receiving any financial support from the partner, since he is also the perpetrator of violence, and having to bear the entire responsibility for the support of any children.

This may drive such women survivors of violence deeper into poverty and also create an intergenerational cycle of poverty. Research from the United States shows that children who grow up in women-headed households experience lower educational and occupational attainment, and girls experience higher risks of teenage pregnancy. Similar results have also been found for women-headed households in Latin America.

Well-paying employment opportunities may be limited for women leaving abusive relationships, because such women have often had their training and educational opportunities restricted by their partners. In addition, battered women may lack the confidence to seek employment or be unable to do so because of their poor health. They may be burdened with medical expenses and legal fees. All of these can contribute to increased financial vulnerability.

Where poverty and gender violence co-exist, the burden on women is immense. For low-income women, limited financial resources affect every aspect of life.

Where and how they live, what they do, who they interact with all these may be severely restricted because of lack of money. They may suffer from poor physical and mental health. In addition, the complex responsibilities of earning a living, maintaining a household and raising children drains them of physical and emotional energy and self-confidence. When gender violence is superimposed on this reality, women may feel trapped and unable to take on the challenge of changing this situation. Many lowincome women stay in abusive relationships because they are economically dependent on their abusers; do not have an alternative place to live; do not have the education or skills to find a job that can support them and their children; often suffer from poor health; and because their self-esteem has been eroded by prolonged abuse or poverty.

Table 2. Estimated global health burden of selected conditions for women aged 15 to 44

Condition	*DALYs lost (millions)*
All maternal conditions	29.0
Sepsis	10.0
Obstructed labour	7.8
STI (excluding HIV)	15.8
Pelvic inflammatory disease	12.8
Tuberculosis	10.9
HIV	10.6
Cardiovascular disease	10.5
Rape and domestic violence	9.5
All cancers	9.0
Breast	1.4
Cervical	1.0
Motor vehicle accidents	4.2
War	2.7
Malaria	2.3

Consequences of Gender-based Violence

GBV affects many women in many parts of the world throughout their life cycles. It gives rise to a wide range of physical and mental health problems including death and disability, making it a major public health concern. Gender-based violence thus perpetuates women's poverty and powerlessness. In this way, gender-based violence is costly not only to its victims, but to society as a whole.

Health consequences of gender-based violence

There is increasing evidence of many negative health consequences of gender-based violence. According to World Bank estimates, rape and intimate partner violence accounted for 5% of the healthy years of life lost to women aged 15-44 years in developing countries. Globally, about 9.5 million disability-adjusted life years (DALYs) were estimated to be lost by women in the reproductive age group, comparable to DALYs lost from tuberculosis, HIV and sepsis during childbirth (Table 1).

The incidence of extreme violence may be limited, but each death associated with gender violence is an avoidable death, usually of a woman who has several years of active life ahead of her.

Physical consequences

Women who have been physically assaulted by their intimate partners often present themselves at hospital emergency rooms or casualty departments, reluctant to admit the true cause of their injury, often reporting it as being an accident. Many others may not be injured seriously enough to need emergency attention, but they receive physical as well as mental scars.

Mental health consequences

The mental health consequences of experiencing gender-based violence, physical, sexual or psychological can be far-reaching. Depression, anxiety and sleeping and eating disorders are common long-term consequences of protracted and long-term violence, as is usual in the case of violence by an intimate partner. Suicidal ideation and suicidal behaviour may also be induced. Episodes of physical and sexual violence may give rise to symptoms typical of post-traumatic stress disorder (PTSD).

Based on her path-breaking research with 435 women who had been in violent intimate relationships, Walker coined the term battered woman's syndrome to describe a set of distinct psychological and behavioural symptoms resulting from prolonged exposure to intimate-partner violence. In diagnostic terms, battered woman's syndrome is the development of characteristic physical, psychological and social abnormalities and symptoms such as depression, low self esteem and isolation which ensue from the direct personal experience of a series of violent acts by an intimate partner. Battered woman's syndrome is now recognised as an implied category of PTSD.

Sexual abuse and rape are physical and psychological violations of an entirely different genre from other kinds of violence. They cause physical injury as well as profound emotional trauma. Survivors of sexual assault often suffer from a variety of trauma-induced symptoms as well as sexual problems. According to one study from the United States of America, women who had been sexually assaulted (including victims of child sexual abuse) were about two times more likely than women who had not experienced sexual assault to qualify for different psychiatric diagnoses, including depression, alcohol and drug abuse, PTSD, obsessive compulsive disorder, generalised anxiety, eating disorders, multiple personality disorder and borderline personality syndrome.

Reproductive health consequences

GBV may also result in fatal and serious nonfatal consequences to women's reproductive health. For example, maternal deaths attributable to gender violence have been reported from studies in South Asia. In a community and hospital based prospective survey of maternal deaths in Western India, almost 16% of maternal deaths were associated with intimate partner violence or violence by a family member. An earlier study carried out in Matlab, Bangladesh had also found that nine per cent of maternal deaths were caused by injuries and violence. A third of these deaths were suicides and 25% were homicides. Violence against pregnant women may also lead to miscarriage and stillbirth.

Sexual abuse, including forced intercourse within marriage and refusal by men to use condoms, puts women at risk of unwanted pregnancy, HIV/AIDS and other STIs. Fear of male reprisal is also a deterrent to use of contraceptive methods by women. Unsafe abortions may result, with potentially serious health consequences.

Negative health behaviours

Victims of sexual violence and abuse may also exhibit a higher prevalence of risk behaviours such as unsafe sex, alcohol and drug abuse, and smoking and eating disorders, which in turn contribute to the already high level of physical and psychological morbidity in women experiencing gender violence. Research has found a higher prevalence of risky sexual behaviours and drug use among adolescents and adults who were abused as children.

Poverty and Gender Concerns in Gender-based Violence

Gender-based violence has serious consequences for

women's health and wellbeing, and for the health of their children. In addition, GBV poses significant costs for the economies of developing countries, including lower worker productivity and incomes, lower rates of accumulation of human and social capital, and the generation of other forms of violence both now and in the future. It is essential, therefore, that every health professional address poverty and gender issues in their work, and also the issue of GBV for reasons of efficiency, equity and human rights.

Efficiency

Efficiency means producing the desired result with the minimum wasted effort. In health, this term refers to better outcomes for health programmes or interventions or a higher probability that desired outcomes will be achieved.

Violence, and women's fear of it, limits women's choices in virtually all spheres of their lives. It detrimentally affects women's self-esteem, their ability to gain an education, earn a livelihood, develop human relationships, and participate in development programmes and in political life. It thus keeps women entrenched in their subordinate position vis-à-vis men, and makes it impossible to escape from poverty.

Gender-based violence may thus be an important barrier to economic and social development. The World Bank's policy research report, Engendering development found strong evidence that gender inequality undermines economic growth and constitutes an obstacle to poverty reduction. Supporting evidence from another World Bank study shows that if the countries of the Middle East, North Africa, South Asia and Sub-Saharan Africa had achieved gender equality in education between the 1960s and 1990s, the income per capita of these countries would have grown by an additional 0.5% to 0.9% per year during that period. For many countries, this would have meant a doubling of their per capita incomes.

Due to its many long- and short-term consequences for women's physical and emotional well-being, the stability of families and the growth and development of children, gender-based violence represents a huge cost to the health care system and to other welfare services. A study at a major United States Health Maintenance Organisation (HMO) carried out in 1991 showed that women who had been raped or beaten had medical costs in à given year that were two and a half times higher than those of women who had not experienced such violence. In another study, 22% of women who had a history of childhood molestation or rape had visited a physician ten or more times a year, compared with only 6 per cent of non-victimised women. Thus, large sums of money are spent on an avoidable and preventable cause of physical and mental ill health.

In Canada, the net lost earnings of battered women unable to work because of assault were estimated at more than seven million Canadian dollars (equivalent to more than five million US dollars) per year, according to an estimate made in 1995. Costs to the welfare system to support women who had left a violent relationship were an estimated 1.8 billion Canadian dollars a year (US$1.3 billion). Costs to the health care system could be comparable or even higher.

In view of the large public health burden represented by gender-based violence, improved population health, improved health program objectives and improved health outcomes could be achieved more efficiently by addressing gender-based violence as an important public health issue.

Equity

Equity in health may be defined as the "absence of

systematic disparities in health (or major social determinants) between groups with different levels of underlying social advantage or disadvantage, such as different positions in the social hierarchy." Inequity refers to an inequality that is avoidable and unfair. In effect, this covers most inequalities and thus the terms are often used interchangeably.

Gender-based violence is a manifestation of gender-power inequalities and perpetuates gender-based discrimination. Achieving gender equity will remain a distant goal as long as gender violence remains unchallenged by public policy, legislation and action. Moreover, evidence suggests that health inequalities (including genderbased ones) are widening. Women, particularly those from low-income or otherwise marginalised or vulnerable populationsare more likely to suffer ill-health than men. This is unfair and avoidable. Ensuring health for all is a matter of social justice or equity. To the extent that these inequalities result from GBV, this problem must be addressed for reasons of health equity.

Human rights

Gender-based violence represents a violation of women's human rights. This has been pointed out in a number of Declarations from United Nations Conferences.

> Gender-based violence and all forms of sexual harassment and exploitation, including those resulting from cultural prejudice and international trafficking, are incompatible with the dignity and worth of the human 56 person, and must be eliminated.

> Violence against women is an obstacle to the achievement of the objectives of equality, development and peace. Violence against women both violates and impairs or nullifies the enjoyment by women of their human rights and 57 fundamental freedoms.

A number of international human rights instruments require States to take effective measures to prevent and eradicate gender-based violence. Several international agreements provide protection to women and girls from violence. These include the International Covenant on Civil and Political Rights, the International Covenant on Economic, Social and Cultural Rights, the Convention on the Elimination of All Forms of Discrimination against Women, the Convention on the Rights of the Child, the Convention against Torture and the Declaration on the Elimination of Violence Against Women. In addition, WHO's constitution lays down the ideal of "attaining the highest achievable standard of health for all'. Ensuring women's right to health will therefore mean implementing programmes and policies for the prevention of gender-based violence and care and treatment for its numerous health consequences.

7

Status of Health Education in India

Sports and Games as a vital component of social and cultural life are embedded in the Indian heritage, and can be found in the archaeological excavations of Mohenjodaro and Harappa, the Vedic literature, the Ramayana and the Mahabharata, the Puranas, the literary works of Kautilya, Kalidasa, Panini and Dandin, as well as in Buddhist and Jain literature. They had been seen as an intrinsic component of education and development of the human personality in the philosophical texts of ancient Greece, the progenitor of the Olympic movement. Every civilisation has evolved and developed its own indigenous modes of physical endeavour and healthy social interaction through a variety of games and sports forms and events. Apart from being a means of physical exercise and fitness, sports and games have been a medium of entertainment, the generation of a spirit of healthy competition, bonding and pride in the community, and an avenue of constructive preoccupation for active young people.

In the modern times, there has been an increasing recognition, at the global level, of the role of sports in development per se. The United Nations brought the theme of 'Sport for Development and Peace' into its agenda in 2001, and issued an inter-agency report in 2003 showing how sports can assist in the achievement of the Millennium Development Goals. Following this report, the General Assembly adopted Resolution 58/5 proclaiming 2005 as International Year of Sport & Physical Education, thus giving a strong impetus to efforts to more fully integrate sports into the development agenda. A series of deliberations/ programmes/activities involving governments, the private sector, civil society and UN agencies during the year identified sports as: i) being integral to quality education with mandatory physical education recognised in a number of countries as a universal pillar to foster education, health and personal development; ii) improving the health standards of the population; iii) achieving sustainable development; and iv) building lasting peace.

The above developments, inter alia, serve to highlight the particular importance of sports as a vital ingredient of the development of youth and children in terms of their education, health and fitness and fostering positive values among them, and the special significance of this when seen in the context of India's demographic profile wherein persons below the age of 35 years constitute nearly 75 per cent of the population - the "Young India" referred to by the Hon'ble Prime Minister in his Independence Day Address. In terms of the imperatives of policy, and priorities for planning and action, this finds expression in the restructured Twenty Point Programme 2006, in which one of the monitorable items under Point No. XIII, Item No. 48 is "Sports for All in Rural and Urban areas".

In terms of the competitive aspects of sports also, there has, over the years, been a sea change, in terms of the manner in which they are played, practiced and perceived at the national and international levels. The standards and levels of endurance, fitness and performance displayed by sportspersons have improved exponentially, the number of competitive sports disciplines has increased with the inclusion of many games indigenous to various regions of the world and, with the massive growth and sophistication in the spheres of media and communications, the visibility of competitive sports has grown enormously.

In tandem with these trends, there has been increasing emphasis on the creation of high quality infrastructure and employment of sophisticated technology in the conduct of sports events, with a great deal of attention being given to the development of advanced scientific and technical support systems for sportspersons. With all this, sports as an area of activity, has acquired vast new dimensions, with multi-faceted implications of an economic nature and business potential also.

Increasingly, hosting of international events is also seen by countries and cities as a means of positioning and show casing themselves in the international arena as tourism, business and investment destinations; significantly, many countries/cities are using these events as an opportunity to revitalise the poorer areas of the cities. The phenomenal growth of satellite television has not only brought international sports events into the bedrooms of billion of viewers across the world, but in the process opened the doors for huge revenue generation through sale of broadcasting rights, advertising, etc.

Equally importantly, these developments have a significant impact on the perceptions and expressions of national aspirations and pride, mass participation, and bringing communities together. The furore in Parliament over the recent poor performance of the India's Cricket and Hockey teams, at one level, and the crowds thronging around television sets to see the Football World Cup in Germany, at another, are testimony to the place that sports have come to occupy in our lives.

The hosting of the inaugural Asian Games in Delhi in 1951 heralded the pioneering role of India in promoting the Olympic movement in Asia, at a time when long colonised and oppressed nations and peoples were beginning to express their independence and aspirations. It is an irony that, at the conclusion of the XV Asian Games in Doha, Qatar, India was in the 8th position, behind Uzbekistan, with a total medal tally of 54 medals (10 Gold, 18 Silver and 26 Bronze), as compared to a tally of 316 medals earned by China, 198 by Japan, 193 by South Korea and 85 by Kazakhstan and at the level of the Olympic Games, we have yet to get a single Gold medal (other than in Hockey in the distant yesteryears) and got a solitary Silver medal in the last Games in Athens.

When it comes to professional excellence at the level of individual sportspersons, it is observed that the consistently rising level of performance in various disciplines is not only related to basic training and grooming at the early stages (which, of course is of vital importance), but is also a product of a complex interaction of scientific back-up comprising, physiological, biomechanical, nutritional and psychological elements, use of state of the art equipments/accessories, adoption of research based modern techniques and a well planned and strict regimen and schedule. During the past two decades several countries, such as Australia and China, have committed substantial financial and human resources to identifying and developing their sporting talent, which is reflected in the exponential growth in their medal tallies in the Olympics and other mega international events. In short, in today's world, an international medal-winner is not just found, or born, but is created through a well-researched, discipline-specific, scientific processes and education, backed up by appropriate incentives. What also emerges from this is that achieving excellence is not something that can come about as a subsidiary activity, but is a full time occupation. This, in turn, has a range of implications in terms of the need for incentives and career options, etc., for talented sportspersons.

India has, of late, been positioning itself as an important host country/destination for organising a variety of multi-discipline, mega, international sports events. After holding the Afro-Asian Games in 2003 at Hyderabad, the World Military Games are proposed to be held at Hyderabad in 2007, the Commonwealth Youth Games will be held in Pune in 2008, followed by the main Commonwealth Games, 2010 in Delhi, and India has also made a bid to host the Asian Games, 2014.

On more than one occasion, the aspiration to host the Olympic Games in India has also been expressed at various levels. While, the hosting of such mega events has a great value in terms of projecting the status and position of the country in the comity of nations, and the legacy, in terms of development and up-gradation of sports and urban infrastructure, together with a variety of other socio-economic spin offs, a major legacy and aim behind the organisation of such games has to relate to development of a sports culture and facilities all across the country, and a significant improvement in the levels of excellence, in terms of performance and medal winning abilities of our sportspersons at the national and international levels. Clearly the present levels of performance and attainment would indicate that much remains to be done in this area, and unless steps are taken in a focused manner, questions could well be raised about the efficacy and desirability of committing substantial resources for staging mega international events.

All this calls for a comprehensive, multi-faceted strategy, and carefully crafted programmes, backed by the allocation of commensurate resources, and a well oiled organisational structure with clearly defined roles for the various stakeholders.

Planning Commission had initially constituted a single Working Group for Youth Affairs and Sports with reference to the formulation of the Eleventh Five Year Plan, and a separate Working Group for the Development of Adolescents. Later, it was decided to constitute a combined Working Group for Adolescents' Development and Youth, and a separate Working Group for Sports and Physical Education. The Working Group held meetings on 21st November, 2006, 27th November, 2006 and 20th December, 2006 to deliberate upon various issues related to planned promotion of sports and development in the country. In its meeting held on 15th January, 2006, the Group extensively discussed the 'Draft Report' and gave final shape to it.

Evolution of Sports Policy

Physical education, games and sports have been receiving attention over successive Plans. During the Second Five Year Plan, the National Institute of Physical Education was established in Gwalior in 1957. In 1961, the National Institute of Sports was established with a vision of promoting excellence in sports up to international standards and a number of steps were initiated towards this end. During various Plan periods emphasis was laid on developing facilities for coaching, promotion of physical fitness programmes, promoting rural sports, development of sports infrastructure, and centers for training and excellence for the sub-junior, junior and senior levels, development of indigenous games, and scouting and nurturing sports talent, including special schemes for the tribal, coastal, hilly and far flung areas with respect to the nurturing of talent in specific disciplines, etc. However, till 1982, sports continued to be looked at as a secondary or a residuary activity under the Ministry of Human Resource Development.

It was only after India hosted the IX Asian Games in 1982 that sports as a subject of policy started receiving attention. In the wake of the Asian Games, 1982, a number of steps were taken in this direction, which included, the creation of a separate Department of Sports under the Ministry of Human Resource Development (MoHRD), which was later expanded into a Department of Youth Affairs and Sports in 1985, and upgraded to a full-fledged Ministry in May, 2000. In 1984, the Sports Authority of India was created as an autonomous registered society under the Department (now Ministry) of Sports. For the first time steps were also initiated for developing a comprehensive, National Sports Policy, and a Resolution in this regard was tabled in both Houses of Parliament on 21st August, 1984.

This led to the National Sports Policy, 1984, and can be seen as the first move towards developing an organised and systematic framework for the development and promotion of sports in the country, and the precursor of the present National Sports Policy, 2001. The Policy, apart from bringing out the need for establishing a network of sports infrastructure and facilities in the rural and urban areas, inter alia, also emphasised the need for making sports and physical education an integral part of the curriculum. This resolve has also been stated in the National Policy of Education (NPE) 1986, which calls for making sports and physical education an integral part of the learning process, and provides for its inclusion in the evaluation of performance. It also underlines the need for making physical education a part of the school improvement programme.

The Preamble to the National Sports Policy 2001 states - "Activities relating to Sports and Physical Education are essential components of human resource development, helping to promote good health, comradeship and spirit of friendly competition, which, in turn, has positive impact on overall development of personality of the youth. Excellence in sports enhances the sense of achievement, national pride and patriotism. Sports also provide beneficial recreation, improve productivity and bolster social harmony and discipline". The twin planks of the Policy are "Broad-basing" of Sports and "Achieving Excellence in Sports" at the National and International Levels.

The Policy states that while the broad-basing of sports will, primarily, remain the responsibility of the State Governments, the Union Government will actively supplement their efforts in this direction and for tapping the latent talent, including in the rural and tribal areas. The Union Government and the SAI, in association with the Indian Olympic Association (IOA) and the National Sports Federations (NSF), will focus specific attention on the objective of achieving excellence at the National and International levels.

The National Sports Policy 2001 set out the framework for the action plan, on the eve of launch of Xth Plan, as follows: -

(a) According high priority to the development of sports in the rural areas by mobilising village panchayats/ gaon sabhas as well as rural youth and sports clubs - (i) to facilitate development of the requisite infrastructure; and (ii) to harness the available talent and potential through an appropriate competition structure in rural areas as also in the disadvantaged and remote parts of the country;

(b) Giving special consideration to the North Eastern Region under various schemes;

(c) Promoting indigenous games;

(d) Actively pursuing the integration of Sports and Physical Education with the educational curriculum, making it a compulsory subject of learning up to the Secondary School level and incorporating the same in the system of student evaluation;

(e) Introducing a National Fitness Programme in all Schools and initiating steps to augment the required resources both material and human;

(f) Setting up of specialised sports schools;

(g) Introducing an appropriate inter-school and inter-college/university competition structure at the National, State and District levels;

(h) Involvement of various agencies, apart from the Government (Central & States), including the Panchayat Raj Institutions, (PRIs), Local Bodies, Educational Institutions, Sports Federations/ Associations, Clubs, Private/Public sector entities and Civil Society for creation, utilisation and proper maintenance of the sports infrastructure at all levels;

(i) Introducing a system of review-based periodic prioritisation of various sports disciplines on the basis of proven potential, popularity and international performance, with a view to put special emphasis on development of such priority disciplines in collaboration with IOA and State Governments;

(j) Setting up centres of excellence to identify and train outstanding sportspersons and sports academies where young and talented sportspersons could be groomed to achieve higher levels of performance in the international sports arena;

(k) Working together of Government, IOA and NSFs in a harmonious and coordinated manner;

(l) Ensuring that the IOA and the NSFs demonstrate orientation towards achievement of results and tangible progress, and their functioning is transparent, professional and accountable;

(m) Preparing Long Term Development Plan (LTDP) for each sports discipline, including a proper calendar of competitions at various levels;

(n) providing the requisite scientific back-up in terms of nutrition, psychology, medicine, pharmacology, physiology, bio-mechanics, anthropometry, etc.;

(o) Initiating suitable measures, including tax-exemptions on imports of raw materials as well as finished goods through OGL route, and sales tax exemptions by State Governments on sports goods, to ensure access to high quality sports equipments;

(p) Taking concerted steps to train Coaches, Sports Scientists, Judges, Referees and Umpires, in line with international standards;

(q) Providing adequate incentives to provide both social recognition and financial security to distinguished sportspersons during and after their sporting careers;

(r) Drawing up joint / unified sports tourism plans for various parts of the country;

(s) Encouraging corporate houses to adopt and support particular disciplines as well as sportspersons through tripartite agreements between the Government, the concerned Sports Federations and the corporate houses;

(t) Encouraging eminent sportspersons to set up sports academies;

(u) Mobilising the electronic media, including the national broadcasters, the private channels and the print media for strengthening a sports culture in the country; and

(v) Pursuing sports exchange programmes with all friendly nations, with emphasis, on the one hand, on advanced training for sports persons and coaches, scientific support, the latest research aids and development of infrastructure, and earning laurels for the country in sports and games, on the other.

The Policy also states that the question of inclusion of "Sports" in the Concurrent List of the Constitution and introduction of appropriate legislation for guiding all matters involving national and inter-state jurisdiction, will be pursued.

In 1987, a Committee, headed by Shri Amrik Singh, was appointed by the Government to study the report of IOA on the performance of India in the Xth Asian Games at Seoul. In 1991, Government constituted another Committee, headed by Shri M. M. Rajendran, to review all the schemes.

The Department-related Parliamentary Standing Committee on Human Resource Development also took up India's performance in international sports as a subject for special study and presented the 34th Report on the subject, covering every aspect of sports, in 1995. The Committee further deliberated on a wide range of issues concerning sports in 1998 vide the Action Taken Report of the Committee. In these Reports, the Committee has, inter-alia, again emphasized the need for bringing about reforms in sports management and governance urgently to make it more dynamic, responsive, responsible and result-oriented.

Some of the problems and issues identified by Committee in their reports are summarised below:

(a) Lack of a sports culture and consciousness in the country;

(b) Non-integration of sports with education;

(c) Lack of proper co-ordination amongst the Centre, States, Federations/Associations and various private and public sector undertakings;

(d) Lack of infrastructure in the rural areas and its concentration in urban/metropolitan centres;

(e) Under-utilisation of available infrastructure and its poor maintenance and upkeep;

(f) Lack of good quality and affordable sports equipments;

(g) Absence of adequate incentives for the youth to take up sports as a career;

(h) Lack of a system for proper identification of talent;

(i) Unfair selection procedure and last minute finalisation of teams;

(j) Lack of adequate exposure and specialised training/coaching of international standards;

(k) Non-availability of nutritious diet for sportspersons;

(l) Inadequate participation of women in sports;

(m) Lack of committed administrators with love and knowledge about sports;

(n) Lack of modern facilities for sports science, sports medicine, psychology, etc.; and

(o) Inadequate allocation for sports in the budget.

Programme Initiatives under the Five Year Plans

The National College of Physical Education and National Institute of Sports were established and sports facilities like stadia, swimming pools etc. were constructed during the Second Plan. The National Coaching Scheme was launched during the Third Plan, while allocations for physical education, games and sports were increased during the Fourth Plan. The Fifth Plan witnessed the expansion of coaching facilities. The Sixth Plan laid emphasis on spotting and nurturing of young talent in different sports and also setting up of facilities at different places for promising sportspersons.

During the Seventh Plan emphasis was laid on development of sports infrastructure at the grassroots level which included laying of synthetic tracks, etc. On the basis of the National Sports Policy framed during Seventh Plan, a Plan of Action was formulated in 1992. During the Eighth Plan, many rural schools were assisted for developing playgrounds and buying sports equipments, and schemes like Special Area Games (SAG) and SPDA were launched with a view to locating and nurturing talented children having potential for sports and to provide specialised training to sportspersons. The Ninth Plan saw a significant step-up in the outlay and laid emphasis on developing excellence in sports, provide modern and scientific facilities including sports physiology and sports medicine, etc. Modern equipments relevant to the training needs of sportspersons were also sought to be provided. During this plan period, the Department of Sports was converted into a full-fledged Ministry of Youth affairs & Sports.

Based on a review of the past experience, the thrust areas identified for the Xth Plan were creation of infrastructure, training facilities, upgradation of coaching skills, promotion of research and scientific support systems, creation of a drug free environment, welfare and incentives for sportspersons, and tapping of resources from the private/public sector and individuals for the development of sports. In addition, keeping in view the observations of the Planning Commission in respect of Zero Based budgeting, the various schemes were sought to be rationalised and brought under the following six categories :

(a) Schemes relating to infrastructure;

(b) Schemes relating to talent search and training;

(c) Schemes relating to holding of National/ International sports events;

(d) Schemes relating to awards;

(e) Scheme relating to institutions; and

(f) Schemes relating to incentives for promotion of sports activities.

Plan allocations for sports from VIth to Xth Five Year Plan are indicated in the following table :-

— VIth Plan - Rs. 26.54 crore

— VIIth Plan - Rs. 207.45 crore

— VIIIth Plan - Rs. 210.00 crore

— IXth Plan - Rs. 472.61 crore

— Xth Plan - Rs. 1145.36 crore

8

Health Education Schemes

Schemes Related to Infrastructure

The Ministry was implementing four Centrally Sponsored infrastructure Schemes during the Xth Plan viz., Scheme of Grants for Creation of Sports Infrastructure, Scheme for Grants to Rural Schools for Purchase of Sports Equipments and Development of Playgrounds, Scheme of Grants for Promotion of Games and Sports in Universities and Colleges, and Scheme of Grants for Installation of Synthetic Playing Surfaces.

Under these Schemes grants were provided to State Governments, Schools, Colleges, NGOs, etc., for creation of sports facilities in accordance with the approved pattern, subject to receipt of viable proposals from State Governments and other agencies.

The Schemes were popular and resulted in the creation of infrastructure facilities like stadiums, sports complexes, swimming pools, etc., at the District, State, School and College levels to an extent. Details of physical and financial targets and achievement under these Schemes are indicated in the following tables:

(i) Scheme of Grants for Creation of Sports Infrastructure including Rural Schools:

Year	Physical		Financial (Rs. Lakhs)	
	Target	Achievement	Outlay	Expenditure
2002-03	450	528	1210.00	1369.00
2003-04	65	182	2000.00	3300.00
2004-05	140	122	2715.00	2755.00
2005-06	-	19	500.00	500.00
2006-07	-	68	3000.00	2807.00
Total XI Plan	655	919	9425	10731

The main logic underlying this was that Sports is a State subject, and the primary responsibility for creating sports infrastructure in the states vests in them. The Ministry had requested the Finance Ministry and the Planning Commission to review the decision in view of the vital importance of the need for establishing sports infrastructure all over the country, and the inability of the States to do this on their own. However, this was not acceded to, and the Planning Commission only agreed to continue funding for committed projects up to the end of the Xth Plan. Apart from persistent demands from the State Governments for revival of the Scheme(s), the Department related Parliamentary Standing Committee has also strongly advocated this, along with a recommendation that there should be better monitoring.

(ii) Scheme of Grants for Promotion of Games and Sports in Universities and Colleges:

Year	Physical		Financial (Rs. Lakhs)	
	Target	Achievement	Outlay	Expenditure
2002-03	120	227	660.00	667.00
2003-04	350	415	1000.00	1087.00
2004-05	475	555	1320.00	1640.00
2005-06	-	10	150.00 1	50.00

2006-07	-	33	150.00	132.00
Total (Xth Plan)	945	1240	3280	3676

(iii) Scheme of Grants for Installation of Synthetic Playing Surfaces:

Year		*Physical*	*Financial (Rs. Lakhs)*	
	Target	*Achievement*	*Outlay*	*Expenditure*
2002-03	5	2	423.00	120.62
2003-04	8	5	470.00	200.00
2004-05	20	4	770.00	150.00
2005-06	-	3	150.00	150.00
2006-07	-	1	200.00	158.00
Total (Xth Plan)	33	15	2013	778.62

As for the actual experience of implementation of these Schemes during the Xth Plan, a major constraint observed pertained to the non-receipt of viable proposals from many States. As a result, the spread of the actual infrastructure proposals sanctioned under the Scheme was uneven and, to that extent, there was also a degree of adhocism in the Scheme.

As far as the Eleventh Plan is concerned, apart from addressing the larger issue of development of sports infrastructure in the country, a view will also have to be taken regarding continued assistance for projects which have been sanctioned in the Xth plan, and could not be completed.

Scheme relating to Talent Search & Training

Under this Scheme financial assistance of up to Rs. 5 lakhs in a year is provided to eminent sports persons for achieving excellence at the international level, and to supporting personnel such as coaches, sports scientists, referees etc. for upgrading their skills, with a view to being able to provide scientific back up and support to promising sports persons. The physical and financial performance under the Scheme during the Xth Plan is indicated in the following table:

Year	*Physical*		*Financial (Rs. Lakhs)*	
	Target	*Achievement*	*Outlay*	*Expenditure*
2002-03	40	37	253.00	Nil
2003-04	40	35	352.00	10.00
2004-05	40	26	340.00	250.00
2005-06	40	55	300.00	39.24
2006-07	36	68	200.00	180.00
Total (Xth Plan)	196	221	1445.00	479.24

The Scheme was a bit slow to take off, but in the last 2-3 years, there has been an increase in the receipt of applications for assistance, which has helped a number of players in achieving excellence at the international level. An analysis of the Scheme, however, suggests the need for more publicity, a more proactive approach vis a vis athletes in Olympic disciplines, increase in the quantum of assistance, greater flexibility, and linkages with other schemes of professional excellence and promotion of medal prospects in international events. Together with this there is also a need to build in a mechanism for monitoring outcomes.

Scheme relating to Events including holding of National/International Sports Events

Guidelines for Assistance to National Sports Federations: Under this Scheme, financial assistance is provided to recognised National Sports Federations (NSF's) for training and participation of teams in international events abroad, organisation of national and international tournaments in India, Coaching and Training of National Teams under Indian and Foreign Coaches with requisite technical and scientific support, procurement of equipment etc.

The objective of the scheme is to enable proper development of different disciplines of sports, the identification of promising sports persons in each discipline, preparation of national teams for participation in international competitions and improving the level of performance and attainment therein. For purposes of assistance under this scheme, guidelines have been formulated to define the areas of responsibilities of the various agencies involved in the promotion and development of sports, to identify NSFs eligible for coverage under the scheme, to set priorities and to detail the procedures to be followed by the Federations to avail Government assistance, and specify the norms of assistance for various activities.

The physical and financial performance under the Scheme during the Xth plan is briefly indicated in the following table:

Year	*Component*		*Physical*	*Financial (Rs. Lakhs)*	
		Target	*Achievement*	*Outlay*	*Expenditure*
2002-03	1	20	50		
	2	30	50		
	3	80	130	3000.00	3948.00
2003-04	1	20	25		
	2	30	45		
	3	80	100	4500.00	2900.00
2004-05	1	20	44		
	2	30	48		

	3	80	105	4831.00	4709.00
2005-06	1	20	120		
	2	30	128		
	3	·80	489	5000.00	4500.00
2006-07	1	20	171		
	2	150	50		
	3	100	122	4500.00	2808.82
Total	1	100	410		
(Xth	2	270	321		
Plan)	3	420	946	21831	18865.82

This Scheme can be viewed as one of the flagship schemes of the Central Government, together with a host of schemes being implemented by the Sports Authority of India (SAI), for the development of sports in the country, with particular reference to the participation of Indian teams in international events. The Scheme has definitely resulted in improvement in the level of performance in various international events like the Commonwealth Games, Asian Games and a number of world and continental championships in different disciplines.

However, in terms of the potential of a country like India, we can ill afford to derive comfort and satisfaction from the results that might have been achieved, and serious consideration would have to be given to the re-orientation of the Scheme in terms of it's constituent elements and prescription of systems to define and monitor outcomes. Inter alia, this will also require a review of the norms and entitlements under different components of the Scheme with reference to aspects like number of exposures and entitlements of athletes, together with basic issues pertaining to the delineation of roles of different stakeholders, and their accountability in terms of results and the objectives to be achieved.

Schemes Relating to Awards

Special Awards to Medal Winners in International Sports Events and Their Coaches: This scheme was introduced in 1986, with the objective of encouraging and motivating outstanding sportspersons for higher achievement and to attract the younger generation to take up sports as a career and strive to achieve excellence. Under the Scheme awards are given by the Central Government to sportspersons and their coaches for winning medals in various international events as per the following scales: -

Name of The Game/ Championship	*Amount*		
	Gold Medal/ First Position	*Silver Medal/ Second Position*	*Bronze Medal/ Third Position*
(i) Olympics Games	Rs. 30 lakhs	Rs. 18 lakhs	Rs. 12 lakhs
(ii) Official World Cups/ Asian /Commonwealth Games	Rs. 10 lakhs	Rs. 5 lakhs	Rs. 3 lakhs
(iii) Asian/ Commonwealth Championships	Rs. 3 lakhs	Rs. 2 lakhs	Rs. 1.5 lakhs

The outlay and expenditure under the scheme during Xth Plan is indicated below:

Year	*Physical*		*Financial (Rs. Lakhs)*	
	Target	*Achievement*	*Outlay*	*Expenditure*
2002-03	NA	NA	250.00	763.00
2003-04	NA	NA	1145.00	2664.00
2004-05	NA	NA	600.00	545.00
2005-06	NA	NA	644.00	400.00
2006-07	NA	NA	594.00	123.00

Total (Xth Plan)	NA	NA	3223	4495

Rajiv Gandhi Khel Ratna Award: The scheme was launched in the year 1991-92 with the objective of giving recognition to, and honouring, outstanding sportspersons, who have distinguished themselves in their field and brought laurels to the country. Under this scheme, an amount of Rs. 5 lakhs is given as award to one sportsperson every year for the most spectacular and outstanding performance in the preceding year.

Maulana Abul Kalam Azad (MAKA) Trophy: Inter-University tournaments are an integral and important part of games and sports in Universities and Colleges which were promoted under the scheme of 'Grants for Promotion of Games and Sports in Universities and Colleges' during Xth Plan. This scheme has been discontinued from 1.4.2005. As an incentive, the MAKA Trophy along with cash award of Rs. 2 lakh is given to winner University in Inter-University tournaments organised through Association of Indian Universities (AIU). In addition, the second and third overall winner universities receive cash award of Rs. 1 lakh and Rs. 50,000 respectively. Although the main scheme of grants to Universities and Colleges has been discontinued, the grant of MAKA trophy was continued during the Xth Plan and is proposed to be continued in the XIth Plan also, while the aspect of inter-university competitions will be considered as part of the 'Competition Structure' proposed to be put up in place during the XIth Plan.

The outlay and expenditure under this Scheme in the Xth Plan is indicated below:

Year	*Physical*		*Financial (Rs. Lakhs)*	
	Target	*Achievement*	*Outlay*	*Expenditure*

2002-03	1	2	7.00	5.13
2003-04	1	1	7.00	6.00
2004-05	1	1	6.00	5.31
2005-06	1	1	6.00	5.10
2006-07	1	1	6.00	5.00
Total (Xth Plan)	5	6	32.00	26.54

Other Awards - Arjuna, Dhyanchand & Dronacharya Awards: In addition to above, Arjuna Award for outstanding performance in sports, Dhyan Chand Award for life time achievement in sports and games and Dronacharya Award for eminent coaches are awarded every year under the Non-Plan Schemes.

Schemes relating to Institutions

Sports Authority of India (SAI): The Sports Authority of India (SAI) was set up in 1984 as a autonomous registered society, and the apex body under the Government of India, for the promotion of sports excellence in the country. The General Body of SAI is Chaired by the Prime Minister, and the administration and management vests in the Governing Body under the Chairmanship of the Union Minister for Youth Affairs and Sports. The Director General, who is appointed by the Government of India, is the Chief Executive Officer of the Authority, with headquarters in Delhi.

Through its different schemes, SAI is engaged in spotting and nurturing talent at the sub-junior, junior and senior levels with the objective of achieving excellence at the national and international levels by providing the requisite infrastructure and equipment, coaching facilities, scientific back up, nutritious diet, and competition exposure, etc. At the commencement of the Xth Plan, SAI had six Regional Centres at Bangalore Gandhinagar,

Delhi, Chandigarh, Kolkata and Imphal, and one Sub-Centre at Guwahati. Since then two Regional Centres have been created at Bhopal and Sonepat and two Sub-Centres at Hazaribagh and Lucknow. Another Sub-Centre has been approved in Tamil Nadu. In addition, through the Netaji Subhash National Institute of Sports (NIS), Patiala (the academic arm of SAI), and some of the Regional Centes, SAI offers a variety of courses in sports coaching and sports medicine(at NIS); and, graduate and post-graduate courses in physical education at the Laxmibai National College of Physical Education (LNCPE), Thiruvanathapuram.

In recognition of its pivotal role in the promotion of sports excellence in the country, the outlay of SAI saw a significant increase in the Tenth Plan. The financial targets for the Tenth Plan have by and large been met. In particular, the expenditure in the last two years of the Plan improved considerably, and unspent balances were also liquidated. The overall position is indicated in the table below:

Year	*Physical*		*Financial (Rs. Lakhs)*	
	Target	*Achievement*	*Outlay*	*Expenditure*
2002-03	NA	NA	9836.00	9836.00
2003-04	NA	NA	12500.00	9808.00
2004-05	NA	NA	14188.00	14435.00
2005-06	NA	NA	15280.00	14355.00
2006-07	NA	NA	16740.00	12423.00
Total (Xth Plan)	NA	NA	68544	60857.00

The qualitative performance of SAI has to be seen in the light of three distinct aspects - Academics, which include the schemes for the training of coaches and other scientific staff, and programmes related to physical education; the activities of SAI, through the TEAMS Division, in collaboration with the NSFs pertaining to the training of identified elite athletes and teams in different disciplines; and Operations which include schemes pertaining to the spotting and nurturing of talent.

Academics -

(a) Netaji Subhash National Institute of Sports (NIS) Patiala

As the premier sports training institution in the country, NIS Patiala has been providing yeomen's service to sports trainers and sportsmen since its inception. It is functioning as the academic arm of the Sports Authority of India (SAI). NIS Patiala, together with its extension centres at Bangalore and Kolkata, conducts a one year Diploma Course in Sports Coaching, the Masters course in Sports Coaching, and the Post Graduate Diploma Course in Sports Medicine. In addition, Refresher Courses and Certificate Course are held at regular intervals in various sports disciplines.

During the 10th Plan period there were 1720 trainees in the Diploma Course, 23 in the Masters Course, and 3453 in the Certificate Course. Special Courses also were conducted for Army Personnel and Foreign Students and 16 persons graduated in the Masters Course in Sports Medicine. While SAI has been offering these basic courses in the areas of coaching and sports medicine, it is felt that there is considerable room for improvement, not only in the teaching methodology and curriculum content, but also in terms of the requirements for teaching staff and faculty at various levels.

It is proposed to set up a high-powered committee of experts and academicians to suggest ways and means to improve the academic and scientific content of the training programmes pertaining to coaching and sports sciences in NIS Patiala before March 2007, so that steps can be taken during the Eleventh Plan to upgrade the systems and arrangements to international standards.

(b) Lakshmibai National College of Physical Education, (LNCPE), Thiruvananthapuram.

(i) SAI also runs the Laxmibai National College of Physical Education (LNCPE) at Thiruvananthapuram, Kerala. The College is affiliated to the Kerala University, and is awarding a three year Bachelors Degree in Physical Education, with an intake of 20 students and a one year PG Diploma Course with an intake of 20 students, per year. During the 10th Plan period, the LNCPE achieved its targets in terms of the number of students admitted. Steps were also initiated to improve the playing infrastructure of the Institute- a new swimming pool was constructed and a new synthetic athletic track is also going to be laid. SAI also runs a training centre (STC) in LNCPE. Some of weaknesses observed in the operations of LNCPE are:

(a) The teaching and administrative faculty requires to be strengthened.

(b) Due to the perceived lack of attractive employment opportunities, the quality of intake into the college has been fairly average. All the candidates applying to this institution come from local areas whereas it is a national institution and should be able to draw students, at least, from the whole Southern region.

(ii) The LNCPE Thiruvananthapuram has a lot of potential to be upgraded into a premier institution in the field of physical education. In this context, discussions have also been held in the Ministry with a view to devising ways to bring synergy in the activities of LNCPE and the Laxmibai National Institute of Physical

Education (LNIPE), Gwalior. It is also proposed that, during the 11th Five Year Plan, special efforts will be made to channelise trainees at the SAI Centres to seek admission under various courses and programmes in LNCPE Thiruvananthapuram or in LNIPE Gwalior.

Towards this end SAI is working more closely with LNIPE, Gwalior to start contact study centres in STCs and SAGs and under the National Open School system to provide Secondary level education to SAI trainees, and then provide the opportunity to whoever wishes to join LNIPE or LNCPE to pursue courses either in physical education or related courses which will have a potential of employability.

Training of Elite Athletes and Management Support (TEAMS) Division: This is the backbone which provides support to the National Sports Federations (NSFs) in the preparation of National Teams which participate in various International events. The TEAMS Division coordinates the Long Term Development Plan of each NSF, provides logistics and training support at NIS Patiala, and other Regional Centres and also at selected training centres outside SAI. The TEAMS Division draws most of its funding from the Ministry under the Scheme of "Assistance to National Sports Federations". The TEAMS Division also provides support to the NSFs in the identification and procurement of foreign coaches and selection of the national coach for each NSF, who is responsible for the training of identified probables for the National teams.

The outcome of these inputs and support from SAI has resulted in a reasonably creditable performance, in comparative terms, in the Melbourne Commonwealth Games 2006, the Doha Asian Games 2006 and in various other Championships. More specifically, very good results have been achieved in the disciplines of Shooting,

Archery, some areas of Athletics, Rowing, Weightlifting, Wrestling, Womens' Boxing and Billiards & Snooker. However, in absolute terms, there is still a very long way to go in terms of reaching a level which can be called satisfactory.

In this context, a number of shortcomings have been identified in the existing arrangements which will need to rectified. These are: -

(i) There needs to be greater focus on scientific and allied support to the national teams during the training;

(ii) Availability of high quality equipments is a continuing gap area though steps were taken to improve the position during the Plan period;

(iii) There has been a shortage of world class coaches for the national teams;

(iv) More focussed attention needs to be given to the development of junior players at the national level together with exposure at the International level;

(v) Infrastructure and personnel support in the area of research and development needs strengthening; and

(vi) The monitoring of the LTDPs requires considerable improvement.

During the 11th Plan period an effort will be made to address all these issues through suitable changes in the scheme of Assistance to National Sports Federations, and the related operations of the TEAMS Division of SAI.

Operations: Schemes for Spotting and Nurturing Talent Different sports promotion schemes of SAI, aimed at spotting and nurturing talent, in different age groups conceived during the VIIth Plan and reviewed/revised during the Xth Plan, are being implemented through the network Centres established by SAI (Sub-Junior (8-14 years), Junior (14-21 years) and Senior (17-25 years).

During the Xth Plan, the number of trainees under the different schemes increased from 7580 to nearly 12000.

(a) National Sports Talent Contest Scheme (NSTC)

(i) The objective of this scheme is to provide an opportunity to talented youngsters and budding sportspersons in the age group of 8-14 years (Sub-Junior) to play and study in a school environment, who on reaching the optimum age can be encouraged to join the system of higher level training for competitive sports. The selection of trainees under the above scheme is done on the basis of potential and performance. Selected trainees are admitted to schools on a non-residential basis. However, in exceptional cases, the trainees are admitted to the schools on residential basis also. The scheme basically envisages identification / adoption of educational institutions having good sports infrastructure as briefly brought out below:-

a) Regular schools: An annual grant Rs.20,000/- is provided to each school for purchase of equipment. In addition, expenses per trainee @ maximum of Rs. 2000/- p.a. for sports kit, Rs. 150/- p.a. for accident insurance and medical expenses, Rs.2000/- p.a. for competition exposure and Rs. 300/- per month stipend for 10 months in a year are provided under the scheme. The schools taken into the scheme are also provided the services of expert coaches for imparting training. 32 schools have been adopted under the scheme out of which 2 schools in tribal areas are residential. In residential schools, trainees are provided Boarding & lodging @ Rs.75 per head per day for 300 days instead of stipend.

b) *Schools having nation-wide chain (Kendriya Vidyalayas, Navodaya Vidyalayas, DAV, Vidya Bharati & other such institutions) for promotion & development of indigenous games & martial arts:* The scheme is based on scouting/retention/weeding out of talent in indigenous games & martial arts on the basis of annual competitions organised by adopted schools through financial assistance from SAI. Annual grants of Rs.25,000/- and Rs. 20,000/- are provided to each school for organising competitions for scouting of talent and for purchase of equipment respectively. Expenses per trainee @ Rs. 1500/- p.a. for sports kit, Rs.150/- p.a. for accident insurance and medical expenses and Rs. 300/- per month stipend for 10 months in an year are given under the scheme. The schools are also provided the services of experts for imparting training to the inmates. During 2002-2003, 27 Schools run by the DAV Management Society and Vidya Bharati Society was adopted under this component of the scheme.

c) *Navodaya Vidyalayas:* Annual grant Rs. 20,000/- is provided to each school for purchase of equipment. In addition, expenses per trainee @ a maximum of Rs. 1500/- p.a. for sports kit, Rs. 150/- p.a. for accident insurance and medical expenses, Rs. 1500/- p.a. for competition exposure and Rs. 300/- per month stipend for 10 months in an year are provided under the scheme, and the schools are also provided the services of experts for imparting training. Till date, 49 Navodaya Vidyalaya have been adopted;

d) Akharas to create a broader base for modern wrestling and supplement the efforts made by various akharas in the country: There are 23 adopted akharas where multi-gym/mat is provided and trainees receive a stipend of Rs. 1000/- per month for 10 months in a year. In addition, 33 upcoming akharas are being provided with multi-gyms/mats.

(ii) The details of number of trainees' schools / Akharas and medals won by the trainees of NSTC for the last three years is given below:

Year	*No. of trainees*	*No. of Schools/Akharas*	*No. of Medals won*	
			National	*International*
2003-2004	2130	99	62	02
2004-2005	2237	99	85	05
2005-2006	2216	131	143	11

(b) Army Boys Sports Company (ABSC)

(i) The Army has joined hands with the Sports Authority of India to nurture and groom talented boys in the age group of 8 to 14 years in 18 Boys Sports Companies. These companies are envisaged as virtual sports schools where sports training with scientific back up and support and facility of education throughout the training period is made available. The objective of this scheme is to tap budding talent and nurture the same with the ultimate aim of improving medal prospects in international sports competitions, by using the excellent infrastructure and disciplined administrative environment in various regimental centres of the Army and, in the process, also provide job security because all the trainees are entitled to an assured career in the Armed Forces. The selection of trainees under the above scheme is done on the basis of performance and potential assessed through a battery of tests. The assistance provided by SAI on a per student basis comprises boarding & lodging charges @ Rs.75/- per day for 10 months; cost of tuition fees, books & stationery, uniform etc. @Rs.1000/- per annum; Sports kit @ Rs.2000/- per annum; Insurance charges @ Rs.150/- per annum; Medical expenses @ Rs.300/- per annum; Competition exposure @Rs.2000/- per annum; and a one time of grant @ of Rs.2000/- per new trainee at the time of admission. In addition, coaches of the allotted disciplines are being provided, and an annual grant @ Rs.50000/- is being provided for maintenance of infrastructure & purchase of sports equipment; The details of number of Centres, trainees and medals won by the trainees of ABSCs in the last three years are given below:

Year	*No. of centres*	*No. of trainees*	*No. of Medals won*	
			National	*International*
2003-2004	08	702	94	20
2004-2005	08	738	21	02
2005-2006	18	830	78	19

(c) SAI Training Centre Scheme (STC)

(i) In 1995, the Sports Project Development Area Centres (SPDA) and Sports Hostel Scheme were merged to create SAI Training Centres (STC). The main objective of the scheme is to train talented/meritorious young sports persons in the age group of 12-21 years (Sub-Junior/Junior) (the age could be relaxed in specific cases based on merit). The STC scheme aims to provide in-house coaching, training and nutritional support to sportspersons who have attained advanced levels of sports proficiency (Medal Winners in District/State or National level Competitions in individual events & participants in

State/ National Level Competitions or medal winners at the District Level in team events) or showing genetic potential in the Olympic disciplines and indigenous sports. The trainees are admitted into the scheme on residential and non-residential basis. A direct expenditure of Rs. 41,550/- per residential trainee per year is incurred under the Scheme, covering Boarding and Lodging expenses of Rs.100/- per day per head for non-hilly areas and Rs.110/- per day per head for hilly areas for 330 days; sports kit @ Rs.4000/-; Competition Exposure @ Rs.3000/-; Educational Expenses @ Rs.1000/-; insurance @ Rs. 150/-; medical expenses @ Rs. 300/- and other expenses @ Rs. 100/-. The non-residential trainees get a Stipend of Rs.6000/- per year in addition to expenses for sports kit and insurance as above.

(ii) The number of Centres has increased from 54 with 4561 trainees in 2002-03 to 57 with around 6000 trainees in 2006. Though this is a core scheme of the Operations Division of SAI, during the Xth Plan some adjustments had to be made by opening some new Centres and closing down certain others which were not functioning properly. This was because the State Governments did not provide the basic infrastructure facilities and hostels as envisaged under the scheme. It was also observed that a number of these Centres could not run in an optimal manner because of lack of proper coaching staff and administrative support. The details of the number of Centres, trainees and medals won by the trainees of STC for the last three years is given below:

Year	No. of centres	No. of trainees	No. of Medals won	
			National	International
2003-2004	58	5465	610	70
2004-2005	57	5502	442	34
2005-2006	57	5790	301	47

(d) Special Area Games Scheme (SAG)

(i) The objectives of this scheme are similar to those of the STC Scheme, but the focus of the SAG Centres is on indigenous games and spotting and nurturing talent in specific disciplines in tribal, coastal and hilly areas, and grooming the same scientifically to achieve excellence in the related modern competitive games and sports. The nature and quantum of financial assistance is the same as that under STC. This scheme has produced very good results since its inception. The SAG Centres are fully funded by SAI, but land has to be provided by the State Governments or other institutions like universities, etc. There were 16 SAG Centres in the year 2002-03 covering 1250 trainees. The number of Centres remains the same but number of the trainees has increased to around 1400 during the Xth Plan period. The details of number of Centres, trainees and medals won by the trainees of SAG for the last three years is as under: -

Year	No. of centres	No. of trainees	No. of Medals won	
			National	International
2003-2004	17	1378	259	37

2004-2005	16	1388	70	6
2005-2006	16	1390	65	4

(ii) The SAG scheme also suffers from the same problems as the STCs viz., shortage of staff and coaches, which is compounded by the fact that they are located in the remote areas of the country, e.g. the SAG Centres in Kokrajhar and Tinsukia (Assam) could only be made operational with great effort.

(e) Centres of Excellence (COX)

(i) As a natural corollary to the schemes catering to the Sub-Junior and Junior levels, the Scheme of Centres of Excellence (COX) has been envisaged to identify and train talented sportspersons and have shown promise at the senior National Competitions in the age group 17-25 years, at the Regional Centres of SAI for nearly 200 days in a year. The trainees are provided with state of the art facilities, equipment and scientific back up along with specialised training. These Centres of Excellence, in fact, operate as regular coaching camps for the best available talent in India and provide two, or possibly three, concurrent layers of highly skilled sports persons in various disciplines, thus giving a wider choice of talent and continuity for later selection to National Teams. Sports persons who attain the best first positions in senior level National Competition, or Junior National Level, sports persons who are at the brink of entering the senior level, and are found to have the potential of making a mark in International Competitions, are admitted into the Centres of Excellence. The scheme has both residential and non-residential options. A direct expenditure of Rs. 36,750/- per residential trainee per year is incurred under the Scheme covering Boarding and Lodging expenses @ Rs.150/- per day per head for 200 days; sports kit of Rs.3000/-;

Competition Exposure @ Rs.3000/-; insurance @ Rs. 150/-; medical expenses @ Rs. 500/- and other expenses @ Rs. 100/-. The non-residential trainees get a Stipend of Rs.9000/- per year in addition to expenses for sports kit and and competition exposure as above.

(ii) SAI is presently running 10 Centres of Excellence in the 6 Regional Centres, the Lucknow Sub-Centre and LNCPE Thiruvananthapuram, and covers only the Olympics disciplines. There were 8 Centres at the beginning of the Plan with 364 athletes, whereafter 2 Centres have been added and the number of trainees has increased to over 400. The performance under the scheme has been as under: -

Year	*No. of centres*	*No. of trainees*	*No. of Medals won*	
			National	*International*
2003-2004	8	371	170	53
2004-2005	8	400	154	43
2005-2006	8	404	121	42

(iii) As mentioned earlier, a number of new Regional Centres and Sub-Centres have been opened during the Xth Plan and, apart from investments in infrastructure and facilities, staff and coaches also had to be drawn from the ongoing schemes of SAI to operationalise these Centres, where substantial other activities of SAI also take place, like training of national teams, etc. It will, therefore, be necessary to provide operational staff to these Regional Centres and Sub-Centres also on same lines as the STCs and SAGs to ensure that they function as fully operational, efficient and independent sports training units.

Sports Infrastructure Development and Capital Works Under this component of its schemes, SAI gives capital grants to its own Regional Centres and to STCs and SAG Centres to develop play fields, hostels, etc. For this Rs. 30-40 crores per annum are spent in the capital budget. During the 10th Five Year Plan period, SAI has initiated steps for laying/replacing synthetic Hockey & athletic surfaces and also for creation of multi-purose halls, Hostel buildings, etc. at a number of Centres. SAI plans to provide international standard training facilities in all its Regional Centres, Sub Centres and major Centres where National Coaching Camps are held.

Central Pool of Technical Equipments

The Scheme provides for the provision of sports equipment and consumables for training of national players selected for various international competitions, and for national sports federations for the conduct of national and international competitions in India. The scheme also aims to equips SAI Regional Centres and Sub-Centres with modern equipment for training of its own inmates. During the 10th Five Year Plan, projects worth Rs.17 crores were implemented for providing State-of-the-Art Equipment, besides setting up modern fitness centres at the major training centres like Patiala, Kolkata, Bangalore and Delhi, which have enabled Indian sportspersons to enhance their performance at the international level. During the 11th Five Year Plan, it is proposed to further upgrade SAI Regional Centres, Sub-Centres and the STC and SAG Centres with the latest training aids and modern sports equipments with the objective of providing to SAI trainees state-of-the-art training facilities.

Laxmibai National Institute of Physical Education (LNIPE)

The Lakshmibai National Institute of Physical Education (LNIPE) was established initially, as a college, on 17th August, 1957, the centenary year of First War of India's Independence. The Institute is located at Gwalior. In recognition of the services rendered in the field of physical education and sports by the Institute, it has been upgraded to a "Deemed University" in 1995. The Institute is an autonomous organisation under the Ministry and is registered under the Madhya Pradesh Societies Registration Act, 1973. The Institute is fully funded by the Ministry of Youth Affairs and Sports, Government of India.

The main objectives are to (i) prepare qualified teachers in the field of Physical Education, Sports/Games and other Inter-Disciplinary subjects; (ii) serve as a Centre of excellence and innovation in the sphere of Physical Education;(iii) undertake, promote and disseminate research and publish literature in this field; (iv) provide professional and academic leadership to other Institutions in the field of Physical Education; and (v) develop and promote programmes of Physical Education and sports and games in Educational Institutions and other organisations.

The Institute runs graduate and post graduate courses in addition to offering M. Phil and Ph.D. programmes in physical education. During the 10th Plan period the BPE course has been upgraded to a four year degree programme, in line with international standards.

The physical and financial performance in respect of the Institute during the Xth Plan is indicated in the following table:

Year	*Target*	*Physical* *Achievement*	*Financial (Rs. Lakhs)* *Outlay*	*Expenditure*
2002-03	490	422	300.00	300.00
2003-04	490	488	475.00	406.50
2004-05	490	457	600.00	450.00
2005-06	535	436	810.00	810.00
2006-07	700	636	1000.00	636.00
Total (Xth Plan)	2705	2439	3185.00	2602.50

The role to be played by LNIPE has to be seen in the context of the overall scenario of the Physical Education sector in the country. Though various Parliamentary Committees and other high powered bodies have, from time to time, reviewed this sector and suggested guidelines and directions for radical improvement in this area, there has not been meaningful progress. At one level, this has serious implications with reference to physical fitness and the potential for sports excellence among the young people as they grow up and, at another, there are implications in the context of job opportunities in the sector which would be mainly in the vast network of educational institutions. There is, however, a silver lining in the burgeoning growth of gymnasiums and health and fitness centers in the hospitality sector, which has increased the demand for Physical Education specialists but, even here the aspect of quality of instructors has to be ensured.

Action will be necessary, particularly at the level of the Ministry of Human Resource Development, in the following areas:

(i) Implementation of the recommendation of NCERT that Health and Physical Education should be a core subject up to class X and an elective subject up to plus two level;

(ii) Improvement in the quality of Physical Education Training and its standardisation by the National Council of Teacher Education, particularly with reference to the mushrooming of institutions in the private sector; and,

(iii) Formulation of strict guidelines for recognition of schools and colleges with reference to mandatory requirement for recruitment of physical education instructors, and provision of playfield infrastructure;

As far as LNIPE is concerned, serious efforts have been made to streamline the functioning of the Institute in terms of personnel management, IT inputs, infrastructure development, etc. During the 11th Plan, LNIPE proposes to set up Regional Centres, and also develop synergy with LNCPE, Thiruvananthapuram and NIS Patiala, and run more tailor made courses, as a part of its response to the situation brought out earlier.

Scheme of incentives for Promotion of Sports Activities

Pension to Meritorious Sports Persons: Under this Scheme, life-time monthly pension, from the age of 30 years, is given to those sportspersons who have won Gold, Silver or Bronze medals in Olympic Games, World Cup/World Championships (in Olympics/Asian Games disciplines) or Gold medals in Asian Games, Commonwealth Games and Para - Olympic Games, provided that at the time of applying for pension, they have retired from an active sports career. The rates of monthly pension under the scheme are as under -

(a) Olympic Games Medal Winners Rs. 5,000/-

(b) World Cups/ Championships Gold Medalist Rs. 4,000/-

(c) World Cups/ Championships Silver/Bronze Medalist Rs. 3,500-

(d) Asian/

	Commonwealth Games	Gold Medalist Rs. 3,500/-
(e)	Asian/ Commonwealth Games	Silver/Bronze Medalist Rs. 3,000/
(f)	Para-Olympics	Gold Medalist Rs. 2,500/-
(g)	Para-Olympics	Silver Medalist Rs. 2,000/-
(h)	Para-Olympics	Bronze Medalist Rs. 1,500/-

The outlay and expenditure during the Xth Plan period is indicated below:

Year	*Physical*		*Financial (Rs. Lakhs)*	
	Target	*Achievement*	*Outlay*	*Expenditure*
2002-03	NA	NA	10.00	20.00
2003-04	NA	NA	20.00	69.00
2004-05	NA	NA	125.00	1700.00
2005-06	NA	NA	650.00	Nil
2006-07	NA	NA	100.00	100.00
TOTAL (Xth Plan)	NA	NA	905.00	1889.00

The basic objective of the Scheme is to provide a degree of financial and social security to sportspersons who have achieved distinction and won laurels for the country in the arena of international sports events. In a sense, this could be seen as an indirect substitute for future career opportunities for talented sportspersons, to give them an incentive to concentrate on sports in their younger years. A review of the Scheme has, inter alia, brought out that the rates of pension had been fixed a very long time ago, and may need to be revised in view of the trends of inflation since then.

A view was also expressed during deliberations that, very few sportspersons may actually be able to get to the stage of winning medals in the international events covered under the scheme, notwithstanding the efforts that may be put in by them by way of pursuing sports as a potential career and, therefore, performance at the national level should also be considered with reference to eligibility under the Scheme. There is also a need for much greater publicity of the Scheme. All these aspects will need to be considered in the 11th Plan.

Rural Sports Programme

This Scheme has been implemented through SAI (acting as an agency on behalf of the Ministry) in coordination with the State Governments. Under the Scheme, grantsin-aid, at the rate of Rs.50,000 and Rs. 25000 per discipline are provided to State Governments /UT Administrations for organising State-level and District level tournaments, respectively. Financial Assistance of Rs.30,000/- per discipline is also made available by the Ministry to Non-Governmental Organisations, including the Nehru Yuva Kendra Sangathan, for organising District-level competitions.. For National-level tournaments, a grant of Rs.2,50,000/- per discipline is provided to SAI for organising the tournaments separately for men and women in various States by rotation. In order to broad-base games and sports in the North-Eastern States, and to tap talent from that area, the Government of India provides a higher level of assistance of Rs.50,000/- and Rs.75,000/- per discipline for district and State-level competitions, respectively.

The position of allocations and expenditure under this Scheme during the Xth Plan is indicated in the table below:

Year	*Physical*		*Financial (Rs. Lakhs)*	
	Target	*Achievement*	*Outlay*	*Expenditure*

2002-03	NA	NA	125.00	71.01
2003-04	NA	NA	1000.00	13.00
2004-05	NA	NA	150.00	135.00
2005-06	NA	NA	309.00	309.00
2006-07	NA	NA	400.00	400.00
TOTAL (Xth Plan)	NA	NA	1984.00	928.01

A review of the implementation of this scheme during the Xth plan brings out that the coverage in terms of organising district and state level competitions has not been satisfactory and, the spread and regularity of such tournaments has been quite uneven. To a considerable extent, this is on account of resource limitations at the level of the States. In addition, there have been limitations at the level of SAI also in terms of its reach and ability to cover each district. SAI has, by and large, been successful in organising national level competitions.

Promotion of Sports and Games in School

The Scheme was introduced in 1986 with a view to raising the standard of sports at the school level, and to encourage their participation in inter-school competitions. Under this scheme, financial grant is given @ Rs. 75,000/- per district and Rs.3,00,000/- per State for holding district and State level inter-school tournaments, respectively. The Sports Authority of India is given assistance @ Rs.2,00,000/- per discipline for conduct of national level tournaments. The School performing the best in the national level tournaments is given an award of Rs.1,00,000/-, along with a rolling trophy. The scheme is implemented through the Sports Authority of India (acting as an agency of the Ministry). The allocations and expenditure under the Scheme during the Xth Plan are indicated in the table below:

Year	Physical		Financial (Rs. Lakhs)	
	Target	Achievement	Outlay	Expenditure
2002-03	NA	NA	233.00	56.00
2003-04	NA	NA	355.00	41.00
2004-05	NA	NA	125.00	125.00
2005-06	NA	NA	412.00	299.59
2006-07	NA	NA	325.00	325.00
Total (Xth Plan)	NA	NA	1450	846.59

A review of the implementation of this scheme during Xth Plan has brought out similar conclusions as in the case of the Rural Sports Programme. Seen together, this brings out the urgent need to review the whole structure of competitions at various levels, without which the objectives of broad-basing sports and having a wide and effective network for spotting talent cannot be achieved.

Sports Scholarship Scheme

This Scheme was launched in the year 1970-71.The aim of the Scheme is to supplement the resources of talented young boys and girls and enable them to have nutritious diet and arrange the necessary basic sports equipment required for them to pursue their sports activities and realise their potential while they pursue their studies. There are the following three categories of scholarships - State level Scholarship (Category -I) @ Rs. 550/- per month i.e. Rs.6600/- per annum; National level Scholarship (Category - II) @ Rs. 700/- per month i.e. Rs.8400/- per annum; and, University/College level Scholarship (Category - III) @ Rs. 850/- per month, i.e. Rs. 10,200/- per annum.

Besides the above, Special Scholarships for Women are also given at the following rates : Scholarship for senior women champions, @ Rs. 1500/-per month, i.e. Rs.

18,000/- per annum; Scholarship for women doing diploma @ Rs. 7,500/- per course; and Scholarship for women doing M. Phil/Ph.D @ Rs. 10,000/- per annum.

The Scheme has been very popular. It provides for an elaborate mechanism for selection of students for entry into the Scheme, and for their subsequent follow -up and monitoring. A number of sportspersons who have achieved distinction at the international level have, in the past, benefited from it. Discussions about the Scheme, however, bring out the need for improving the database and considerably strengthening the monitoring and follow-up mechanism.

The physical and financial performance under the Scheme during the Xth Plan is indicated in the table below:

Year	*Physical*		*Financial (Rs. Lakhs)*	
	Target	*Achievement*	*Outlay*	*Expenditure*
2002-03	4727	6533	394.00	394.00
2003-04	7480	8083	500.00	507.00
2004-05	8000	9158	450.00	550.00
2005-06	7000	9168	729.00	586.00
2006-07	8000	8000	500.00	500.00
TOTAL (Xth Plan)	35207	40942	2573.00	2537.00

National Sports Development Fund:

The National Sports Development Fund was set up in 1998 with a view to mobilising resources from the Government as well as non-governmental sources, including the private/corporate sector and non-resident Indians, for the promotion of sports and games in the country. In order to make contributions to the Fund attractive, 100% exemption from Income tax has been provided for.

The Government had made an initial contribution of Rs.2 crores during the year 1998-99; and has provided additional funds in subsequent years. Under the scheme Government is committed to contribute to the fund on a matching basis with reference to contributions received from other sources. The monies available in the Fund are intended to be applied for the promotion of sports in general, and specific sports disciplines and individual sports persons in particular, for achieving excellence at the National and International level.

The response of the non-governmental sources in terms of contributions to the Fund has, however, been very lukewarm, and till date it has been able to generate a very small amount of around Rs. 6.00 crores only, most of it by way of contributions by the Government. The outlay and expenditure under the Scheme during the Xth Plan is indicated in the table below:

Year	*Physical*		*Financial (Rs. Lakhs)*	
	Target	*Achievement*	*Outlay*	*Expenditure*
2002-03	NA	NA	100.00	Nil
2003-04	NA	NA	150.00	19.50
2004-05	NA	NA	50.00	Nil
2005-06	NA	NA	100.00	30.00
2006-07	NA	NA	25.00	25.00
TOTAL				
(Xth Plan)	NA	NA	425.00	74.50

The Fund has so far been mainly used to provide assistance to individual sportspersons for their specific requirements related to training and equipments, etc., which has yielded good dividends in the form of performance and medals in international events This is an excellent scheme. Among other things, it also provides a great deal of flexibility in terms of possible utilisation of funds for a variety of purposes related to the promotion and achievement of sports excellence. However, as mentioned earlier, adequate participation of the corporate sector has not been forthcoming, and there appears to be considerable scope for utilising the Fund more optimally and effectively. There is also need for greater publicity and dissemination of information about the Scheme both among sportspersons and the corporate sector. These issues will need to be addressed in the 11th Plan.

Scheme of State Sports Academy

This Scheme was launched with the objective of promotion of excellence through the creation of a state-of-the-art structure, in a Public-Private Partnership framework, for selection of the best available sports talent in the age group of 10-13 years; scientifically groom them over the years of Secondary and Senior Secondary Schooling; and carry this proven and tested potential to the College level. Under the Scheme, it is proposed to establish in every State/UT one Sports Academy with one major discipline out of the athletics, football, hockey (men and women) and wrestling, and any discipline selected by the promoters. The scheme provides for joint funding by the Central Government, State Government and a private sponsor, in a ratio of 25:24:51 subject to the Central Government contribution being restricted to (i) a maximum of Rs.218 lakhs or 25% of the capital/non-recurring cost whichever is less; and (ii) recurring grant being restricted to 25% of actual recurring cost subject to maximum of Rs.17 lakhs per annum for a period of three years.

The total requirement of funds for one academy has been restricted to a ceiling of Rs.968 lakhs. Though 1-2 proposals were identified, not a single project has actually materialised, apparently because the basic framework has not been realistically conceived. As a result, there was no expenditure under the Scheme against an outlay of around Rs. 28 crores during the Xth Plan. Some initial discussions have been held with representatives of the corporate sector as part of the deliberations of the Working Group, and it is proposed to continue this Scheme in the 11th Plan after reformulating it on the basis of more detailed discussions with all stakeholders.

Scheme for Dope Test

This scheme was launched with the objective of establishing an IOC accredited Dope Control Centre in India; educating sportspersons, coaches and other connected personnel about the ill-effects of doping and regarding anti-doping measures; conducting in-competition and out of competition dope tests on sportspersons; and, harmonising various doping related measures with international regulations and prescriptions of the World Anti Doping Agency (WADA). During the Xth Plan, the Scheme has been run through SAI. The process of establishing a self-contained autonomous mechanism, compatible with international regulations is now underway.

During the Xth Plan, a state-of the art laboratory has been set up which is under the process of WADA accreditation; India has signed the Copenhagen Declaration on Anti- Doping; and a National Anti Doping Agency (NADA) has been constituted during the Xth Plan. All these activities will be consolidated and carried to a logical conclusion during the 11th Plan. The position in respect of the outlay and expenditure during the Xth Plan is indicated in the table below:

Year	*Physical*		*Financial (Rs. Lakhs)*	
	Target	*Achievement*	*Outlay*	*Expenditure*

2002-03	Nil	Nil	150.00	150.00
2003-04	Nil	Nil	150.00	415.00
2004-05	Nil	Nil	720.00	445.00
2005-06	Nil	Nil	940.00	Nil
2006-07	Nil	Nil	400.00	400.00
TOTAL (Xth Plan)	Nil	Nil	2360.00	1410.00

Scheme of Commonwealth Games 2010

During the course of the Xth Plan, India's bid to host the XIX Commonwealth Games (CWC) was accepted by the Commonwealth Games Federation (CGF). The Games will, accordingly, be held in Delhi from 3rd to 14th October, 2010. As a sub-set of the CWG-2010, the Commonwealth Youth Games (CYG) will also be held in Pune, Maharashtra, in 2008. There will be 17 disciplines, comprising Aquatics, Archery, Athletics, Badminton, Boxing, Cycling, Gymnastics, Hockey, Lawn Bowls, Net Ball, Rugby 7's, Shooting, Squash, Table Tennis, Tennis, Weightlifting and Wrestling, in the CGW-2010, and 9 disciplines comprising Athletics, Badminton, Boxing, Table Tennis, Tennis, Swimming, Weightlifting and Wrestling in the CYG - 2008. Around 7500 and 1500 athletes and connected sports officials, respectively, from 71 countries are expected to participate in these Games.

The major elements involved in the preparations for, and conduct of, the Games include the establishment of the required sports venue and other related infrastructure, the establishment of a Games Village for the CGW-2010, technical and administrative arrangements for the conduct of the Games, the necessary security arrangements, and up-gradation of the civic infrastructure.

In addition, steps will also have to be taken for the preparation of teams for the Games with a view to enhancing the Indian medal prospects in the Games. While the responsibility for the establishment of the sports and other infrastructure directly related to the conduct of the Games, preparation of the teams, and the security related arrangements, lies mainly with the Central Government, the responsibility for the conduct of the Games vests in an Organising Committee, which has been set up as a registered autonomous body, and the Government of NCT of Delhi (GNCTD) is responsible for up-gradation of civic infrastructure in Delhi.

As per decisions taken at the level of the Core Group of Ministers (GOM), set up under the chairmanship of the Union Minister for Human Resource Development, to coordinate arrangements for the Games, the required sports venue infrastructure is to be established mainly by the Sports Authority of India (SAI), with some venues having been allotted to the Delhi Development Authority (DDA) and the GNCTD/NDMC. The responsibility for developing the Games Village has been given to the DDA and, to the extent possible, is to be developed on a Public-Private Partnership basis.

For purposes of financial allocations, the Ministry of Youth Affairs and Sports will be responsible for the sports venue infrastructure allotted to the SAI, and for the Tennis venue allotted to All India Lawn Tennis Association (AITA), the special arrangements that may be required for preparation of teams for the Games, and the funds to be provided to Organising Committee for the conduct of the Games. In addition, funds are proposed to be provided, through the budget of the Ministry of Youth Affairs and Sports to the State Government of Maharashtra for the sports infrastructure for the CYG-2008 in Pune.

Funds for the infrastructure to be developed by the DDA are to be provided from the budget of the Ministry of Urban Development, for the security arrangements from the budget of the Ministry of Home Affairs, and for the civic infrastructure though the Plans of the GNCTD and the Jawahar Lal Nehru National Urban Renewal Mission (JNNURM).

The funds to be provided to the Organising Committee would be on a "Revenue Neutral" basis, on the assumption that the conduct of the Games would generate sufficient revenues through sale of broadcasting rights, advertising, sponsorship, merchandising, and ticketing, etc.

The position of the outlays and expenditure in respect of the Commonwealth Games during the Xth Plan is indicated in the table below :

Year	*Physical*		*Financial (Rs. Lakhs)*	
	Target	*Achievement*	*Outlay*	*Expenditure*
2005-06	NA	NA	4550.00	3305.00
2006-07	NA	NA	15000.00	8108.00
TOTAL (Xth Plan)	NA	NA	19550.00	11413.00

So far, an amount of Rs. 112.50 crores has been provided to the Organising Committee for meeting international commitments in terms of the Bid Document and the Host City Contract signed between the CGF and the Government of India, GNCTD and the Indian Olympic Association (IOA) and the requirements of the Organising Committee, and Rs. 12.50 crores has been provided to SAI in the context of the venue infrastructure works allotted to it. These funds have been provided on an ad-hoc basis, keeping in view the recommendations of the Expenditure Finance Committee (EFC) in the Ministry of Finance.

The outlays during the Xth Plan were provided on the basis of initial preliminary estimates projected at the stage when the proposal to bid for the CWG - 2010 was being considered by the competent authority. Subsequently, detailed exercises have revealed that the initial cost projections were considerably under estimated, and had been made without fully going into the details of the likely actual requirements of the infrastructure and other arrangements for the Games. Since then, detailed financial estimates for the various components have been prepared/are under preparation, based on which proposals for the Eleventh Five Year Plan are being made.

The position mentioned above also brings out the need for clear schematic guidelines in respect of proposals to host any mega-international events, which could call for expenditure and other arrangements which do not fit into any other specific scheme of the Ministry, and would require additional outlays.

In this context, it may also be mentioned that, in 2005, the IOA had also put up a proposal to bid for hosting the XVII Asian Games, 2014 in Delhi, and again the estimated expenditure on various elements was indicated on an adhoc basis. While approval to put in the bid was accorded, it was also decided that detailed proposals regarding the financial implications and institutional arrangements should be worked out and put up for approval of the competent authority. While this is being done, it has also been observed that there is no specific scheme under which expenditure on pursuing the bid process in such cases can be met. These aspects are proposed to be dealt with suitably during the Eleventh Plan.

9

Physical Education Scenario

Under the Constitution of India, 'Sports' figures at Entry No. 33 in List II (i.e. State List) of the Seventh Schedule of the Constitution under "Theatres and dramatic performances; cinemas subject to the provisions of Entry 60 of List I; sports, entertainments and amusements". It would appear from this that, in a system sense, the whole subject of Sports is still seen in a very limited manner and context.

At another level, this has created limitations with reference to the roles of key stakeholders viz., the States and the Centre, which have worked against a holistic approach and system geared to the promotion and development of sports in a comprehensive manner.

The Sports Policy states that the objective of broad-basing sports will primarily remain the responsibility of the States, and the Central Government, while supplementing their efforts in this direction and for tapping the latent talent, will focus specific attention on the objective of achieving excellence at the National and International levels in coordination with SAI, IOA and the National Federations.

In so far as the role of supplementing the efforts of the State Governments in the sphere of broad basing of sports is concerned, it could be said that, this has been substantially withdrawn with the transfer of the sports infrastructure related schemes to the states during by Xth Plan. In turn, the allocation of resources for sports by the State Governments has, at best, been peripheral and marginal. At yet another level, a third set of key stakeholders, viz., the National Sports Federations, are neither within the jurisdiction of the states, nor has any effective and meaningful regulation in a systematic manner been possible from the Central level, since "Sports" is a state subject.

All these factors have led to a situation in which the various measures that have been taken so far, tend to become stand alone measures, which do not fully fit into a comprehensive and integrated conceptual framework. This situation is also reflected in the implementation of various schemes of the Ministry as briefly analysed and reviewed earlier.

In order to develop a comprehensive framework for the development of sports in a holistic manner, it would need to be seen in a three fold perspective - the development of sports and physical education as an essential ingredient of youth development and promotion of a sports culture in the country; broad-basing of sports in the context of the new dimensions that sports as an activity, per se, has acquired and the opportunities that it could provide for our youth; and, promotion of excellence, particularly with reference to competitive sports at the international level.

The approach and strategy for the Eleventh Plan would have to be formulated and implemented keeping in view the following conceptual framework and thrust areas, and the requirements flowing from the same :

Approach & Strategy for the XIth Plan

Broadbasing of Sports

— Access to organised sports and games facilities for children and youth in rural and urban areas;

— Availability of playgrounds/playing surfaces;

— Creation of necessary sports infrastructure from grass-roots level upwards;

— Development of a structure of competitive events at different levels for promoting a broad-based sports culture and enabling talent search on a large-scale; and

— Involvement of educational institutions in this process, in a structured manner from the primary school level to the University level.

Promotion of Sports Excellence:

— Evolving a structured system for spotting talent at various levels and significantly increasing the pool of talented sportspersons in all Olympic disciplines and identified indigenous sports;

— Focussed attention, in the above context, to areas and regions having potential of excellence in the specific/identified disciplines;

— Establishing infrastructure and an integrated framework for provision of training and grooming of talent at different hierarchical, age and proficiency levels, involving SAI, State Governments and NSFs;

— Active involvement of the corporate sector in developing academies and centres of excellence for different disciplines;

— Expanding and improving coaching facilities, including development of high class, international level, coaches for different disciplines;

— Strengthening scientific and technical support systems and facilities for development of sports and sportspersons; and

— Ensuring the availability of quality sports goods through imports and development of the indigenous sports goods industry.

— Involvement of the media in popularisation and broad basing of sports.

Improvement in Performance at National/international Level

Together with various steps for the promotion of excellence in sports, which would be expected, inter alia, to lead to higher levels of performance and achievements at the national level, and a larger pool of probables for international representation, measures would be required to ensure significant improvement in the performance of Indian sportspersons in the international arena.

This would call for review and re-orientation of systems and procedures pertaining to identification of probables, coaching and organisation of camps, including close monitoring and follow-up, timely selection of teams based on objective criteria, provision of scientific back-up and support during training/coaching camps and at the competition stage, and organised debriefing and monitoring of outcomes.

This would call for clear delineation of the roles and responsibilities of the related organisations/institutions, viz., SAI, IOA and NSFs, together with action to co-opt the private sector in the form of adoption of disciplines/ teams, sponsorship, etc., to supplement the efforts of the Government, SAI and NSFs.

Incentives to Sportspersons: This is an essential corollary to the promotion of excellence and would comprise the following complimentary elements :-

— Awards and recognition;

— Development of a framework for creating career/job opportunities for sportspersons, including utilisation of services of individual sportspersons in other sports related activities through re-orientation, re-skilling, etc.

— Creation of supplementary avenues for subsistence and social security through pensions, etc. for retiring sportspersons;

The strategy is to cover larger number of outstanding sportspersons under the related schemes.

Institutional Framework: Close coordination and convergence would be required in the activities of the key stakeholders, viz., Central and the State Governments, SAI and the NSFs. This would inter alia, require the following action :

(a) State level activities/programmes and responsibilities would need to be clearly delineated, (including inventory and documentation of state level facilities and infrastructure), integrated with the national agenda/programme, and monitored periodically.

(b) The facilities under SAI would need to be systematically and scientifically expanded, upgraded and streamlined. Together with this, management aspects pertaining to development of different individual sports disciplines will also need to be reviewed and made more effective.

(c) Roles and Responsibilities of NSFs would need to be clearly defined to make them more professional, focused, result-oriented and accountable. The concept of having a MoU with NSFs would also need to be considered in this context.

Bringing Sports under Concurrent List: With reference to the emerging dimensions of sports as an important social sector and its inherent linkages with the education system, the vital need for integrated institutional arrangements for the development and promotion of sports in the country, and the evolving profile of sports in the international context, it will be necessary to pursue, and build a consensus on, the proposal to bring "Sports" in the Concurrent List.

Physical Education and physical fitness: Physical education and physical fitness has to be promoted as a national agenda through an integrated approach as outlined below:

(a) Implementation of the recommendation related incorporation of Physical Education and sports in the educational curriculum with the support of the Ministry of HRD and the State Governments;

(b) Motivating, supporting and facilitating educational institutions to give focused attention to physical education;

(c) Modernisation of LNIPE and expansion of its activities.

Framing Specific Policy regarding mega/multi sporting events: A scheme relating to organisation of mega/multi sporting events such as Olympics, Asian Games, Commonwealth Games, World Championships, etc. in India would need to be formulated to spell out the process from the bid stage onwards, role and responsibilities of various stakeholders, aspects related to resource mobilisation, monitoring mechanisms, etc.

Anti-doping measures/programmes: Considering the growing menance of doping in the context of performance related pressures among sportspersons, focused measures will be necessary, including a focused anti-doping education campaign, development of Test Management Plans, putting in place Result Management Mechanisms, and ensuring quality testing of samples, etc. Inter alia, this would also involve operationalisation of the National Anti Doping Agency (NADA) and getting WADA accreditation for the National Dope Test Laboratory.

Promotion of Sports among persons with Disability: The Olympic and Commonwealth Games movement has made promotion of and events related to persons with disability an integral part of the main events. The National Policy recognises that Persons with Disabilities are a valuable human resource for the country and seeks to create an environment that provides them equal opportunities, protection of their rights and full participation in society. In the recent past, the performance of Indian Elite Athletes with Disability (EAD) has been impressive at the international level. A comprehensive scheme needs to be formulated to ensure planned and systematic promotion of excellence in this field during XIth Plan. A Committee constituted by the Ministry in this regard is in the process of finalisation of its report.

Involvement of the Corporate Sector in the Development of Sports: A comprehensive and multifaceted strategy would need to be formulated for corporate sector participation and involvement in the development and promotion of sports. This could include involvement in talent spotting and nurturing; creating sports infrastructure; setting up centers of excellence/academies; establishing sports science labs; adoption of disciplines and sponsoring of individuals & teams, etc.

Recommended Programmes and Action During XIth Plan

The proposals and recommendations of the Working Group for the XIth Plan, in respect of the various key policy and functional areas have been formulated in the light of the perspective, approach and strategy outlined in the preceding chapters and are brought out in the

Broadbasing of Sports

Broadbasing of Sports is key to the promotion and

development of sports, and development of a sports culture in India, and in the long run for enhancing our performance at the national and international level in a sustained manner. In order to do this, it is necessary to make available, in a systematic manner, playing surfaces and facilities at all levels throughout the country, encourage young people, in and out of school, to participate in games and sports as an essential part of their daily life and routine, develop an integrated structure of competitive sports from the grassroots to the national level, and put in place a multi-tiered system of talent spotting and nurturing.

Over the years, under various schemes of the Central and State Governments, a variety of sports infrastructure facilities have been established, particularly at the district level and above, and some State Governments are also implementing schemes for establishing facilities at the village level also. However, the spread of these facilities is uneven, and there are clear gaps in the extent and manner of utilisation of these facilities and the conduct ot competitive events, particularly at the sub-district level, which inevitably also limits the opportunities for both the throwing up and spotting of talent.

It is proposed to launch a major new scheme under the title of "Panchayat Yuva Khel Abhiyan" for filling up the gaps at the sub-district level, and to re-orient the existing schemes of Rural Sports Programme and Promotion of Sports and Games in Schools with the aim of developing a comprehensive competition structure up to the national level.

Panchayat Yuva Khel Abhiyan

The objective of the scheme is to identify and provide playgrounds and create basic infrastructure and facilities for sports and games at the village and block levels, generating a sports culture by ensuring organised access to such facilities for the rural youth, organisation of competition and non-competition sporting activities at the village level, and developing a competition structure up to the district level.

The scheme is proposed to be implemented by, and with the fullest involvement of, the Panchayat Raj Institutions and the Rural Youth and Sports Clubs established under the aegis of the Nehru Yuva Kendra Sangthan (which presently number around 2.5 lakhs in the country), and any other schemes of the State Government, etc. It is expected that, over a period of time, this could also lead to the development of a sports club culture.

Linkages will be established with other institutions and organisations viz. the Sports Authority of India, the State Sports Departments, and the Sports Associations for purposes of basic training/capacity building of grassroots functionaries in respect of organisation of events, managing the facilities and spotting of talent, and, at another level, with reference to the organisation of competitions which can get integrated with the higher level competition structure at the district, state and national levels.

A considerable degree of flexibility is proposed to be provided under the scheme by way of deciding the particular games and sports to be taken up at the village level, and the nature of the infrastructure to be developed, subject to broad schematic guidelines and basic norms and parameters. For purposes of funding under the scheme, it is proposed to bring in the greatest possible synergy and convergence between various schemes of the Central Government, such as the National Rural Employment Guarantee Scheme, Backward Regions Grant Fund, relevant schemes of the Ministry of Tribal Affairs and Department for the Development of the North Eastern Region, M.P. Local Area Development

Scheme, funds available to the PRIs through devolution, and the schemes of the State Governments for development of sports infrastructure. This also implies that the basic process of planning and formulation of proposals would have to be decentralised to the village and block levels.

Keeping in view the diversity of sources of funds for the scheme, and the differences which would inevitably be there in terms of the type of sports infrastructure that can be created in different villages with reference to land availability, and facilities already available, the scheme is proposed to be designed with an approach of incentivisation, whereby funds would be provided on the basis of certain fixed criteria for creation of infrastructure facilities, procurement and maintenance of equipments/ accessories, and organisation of games and sports activities, including honorarium for volunteer organiser/ coordinator.

The following assistance is proposed to be provided under the Scheme, subject to specific proposals to be developed at the district level on the basis of village and block levels plans:

— A one-time grant of Rs. 50,000 to each village panchayat (Rs. 75,000 for NE states, J&K, HP & the hilly areas of Uttranchal) to undertake, in conjunction with other employment-generation and asset-creation schemes, the preparation/ development/improvement of an identified playground/ waterbody/indoor hall, etc.;

— A one-time grant of Rs. 100,000 to each block panchayat (Rs. 150,000 for NE States, J&K, HP and hilly areas of Uttranchal) to undertake, in conjunction with other state and central schemes, the preparation/ development/ up-gradation of an identified playground/waterbody/indoor hall etc.;

— An annual grant of Rs. 10,000 for the acquisition and maintenance of equipments/accessories and support fixtures including consumables to each participating village panchayat and block Panchayat;

— A recurring grant of Rs. 12,000 per annum be given to every participating village panchayat for undertaking various sporting activities, including payment of honorarium to volunteer/trainer.

— A recurring grant of Rs. 24,000 per annum to every participating block panchayats for undertaking sports activities, including payment of honorarium to volunteer/trainer.

— Award of Rs. 25,000, Rs. 15,000 and Rs. 5,000 respectively to Village Panchayats, setting the 1st, 2nd, 3rd position in the block competitions, to be used for promotion of sports and games in a manner decided by the Gram sabha;

— Award of Rs. 50,000, Rs. 30,000 and Rs. 10,000 respectively to the Block Panchayats, setting the 1st, 2nd and 3rd position in the annual district competitions, to be used for promotion of sports and games in a manner decided by them.

Competition Structure

As brought out earlier, the implementation of the schemes pertaining to the "Rural Sports Programme" and "Promotion of Sports and Games in Schools" has been uneven and, in fact, during the deliberations of the Working Group, it became clear that it has been patchy, with no organised linkages with any kind of structure related to talent spotting and selection for higher level training and representation of sportspersons participating in competitions organised under these Schemes. While it was recognised during the deliberations that there would be limitations, particularly in the Rural Sports

Programme, with reference to the degree of professionalism that could be there in these competitions in terms of the national and international norms, restrictions and regulations, and they would have to be viewed substantially as channels for simply encouraging participation in sports and games, it was also recognised that lateral and hierarchical linkages of these programmes with the system of more formal competitions and selections in the State and National teams cannot be ignored. It was felt during the deliberations that the existing schemes of the "Rural Sports Programme" and "Sports and Games in Schools" should be continued with some modifications.

Programme of Rural/Open Sports Competition

The main features of this Scheme in the Eleventh Plan are proposed to be as under:

— In terms of coverage for purposes of participation, it would cover rural as well as municipal/urban areas.

— The competitions would be multi-sport events, with a certain number of Olympic disciplines being made mandatory and some indigenous disciplines could be selected on an optional basis.

— Funding would be done directly on a consolidated basis to the State Governments rather than on a discipline-wise basis through the SAI, and will be based on State Government proposals bringing out an annual calendar of events.

— The tournaments would be held at the district level, followed by one tournament at the state level.

— The district level tournaments will be organised by an Organising Committee, in which the representatives of the State Sports Department (convener), the district administration, the Sports Associations, SAI, the Zila Panchayat and other local bodies, and the Nehru Yuva Kendra Sangathan (NYKS) will be involved.

— Similarly, at the State level, an appropriately constituted Organising Committee would conduct the tournaments.

Promotion of Sports and Games in Schools

The salient features of this Scheme in the Eleventh Plan would be broadly similar to those brought out in respect of the Programme for Rural/Open Sports Competitions. The tournaments would be organised by the State Governments through the Department of Education in close coordination with the State Sports Department, and would be held at the District and State level. The funding will also be done directly to the State Governments, based on proposals containing a calendar of events and other relevant details.

As would be seen, under both the above Schemes, tournaments are proposed only up to the State level, whereafter, it is expected that the promising sportspersons emerging from these events, would be picked up and included in the State teams for the national level tournaments to be organised by the National Sports Federations for each discipline under their programme for holding district, state and national tournaments. As far as national level School Games are concerned, it is proposed that the School Games Federation of India would be considered as another Federation for this purpose and financial assistance provided to them.

At present, there is no structured system for holding of Inter-University Competitions, since the Scheme of Grants for Promotion of Games and Sports in Universities and Colleges was a part of the infrastructure schemes, which was transferred to the state sector with effect from

1.4.2005. As a result, the Association of Indian Universities (AIU) is organising Zonal and National Inter-University Competitions from time to time, but they do not have any linkages with other sports bodies. It is proposed that, in the Eleventh Plan, as a logical extension of School Games, the organisation of Inter-University Competitions at the Zonal and National Levels, would be revived, as an important component of the overall structure of competitions in the country, with the necessary linkages in terms of technical support being provided by the National Federations, and performance based identification/selection of sportspersons participating in these competitions for purposes of further training and representation at the national and international levels.

It is proposed that the national level competition structure should have the following components :

(a) *National Competitions:* These should essentially comprise: (i) discipline wise annual national championships for Sub-Junior, Junior & Senior levels organised by the National Sports Federations (NSF) under the scheme of assistance to NSFs; (ii) Annual National School Games to be organised by the National School Games Federation of India/SAI; (iii) Annual National University Games in identified Olympic and indigenous disciplines to be organised by AIU; and (iv) National Games organised every two years by IOA in collaboration with the host state/s.

(b) *International Competitions:* In addition, keeping in view the advantages that can accrue from international exposure at home, as also to add further value to sports promotion measures in the country (and in the process also enable fuller utilisation of the sports infrastructure being created), the Ministry will encourage and support NSFs to organise officially recognised, discipline specific international events, including prize money events, in certain disciplines such as Tennis, Table Tennis, Badminton etc., in India with the support of International Federations. For the purpose of prize money, the Federations concerned would need to enlist active collaboration of the corporate sector.

(c) Each NSF will be required to prepare and publish an integrated annual competition calendar well before the commencement of the year.

Talent spotting

As brought out earlier, the main schemes for Talent Search and nurturing at present are the Scheme of Talent Search and Training, implemented directly by the Ministry of Youth Affairs & Sports, and the National Sports Talent Contest Scheme being implemented by the Sports Authority of India. The former is, in fact, not directly related to talent search, but relates to provision of financial assistance to sportspersons who have already attained a certain level of achievement to enable them to further improve their performance at the international level, while the latter also requires considerable fine-tuning and development of linkages with an institutionalised system of talent search going down to the grassroots level, while retaining its basic current components.

A review of various relevant Schemes run presently by SAI, which would be relevant from these angles brings out the following :-

(i) The National Sports Talent Contest Scheme (NSTC) is, by and large, the only Scheme in which children from the sub-junior level upwards would be covered (except in the case of Akharas), and this is being done by adoption of schools of different categories and, within them, admission/adoption of students who have displayed meritorious performance as per the criteria of selection.

(ii) In so far as, the SAI Training Centres (STCs) and Special Area Games (SAG) Centres are concerned, generally junior/senior level trainees only come into these, because of inherent difficulties in being able to tie up arrangements for the education of younger boys and girls, and reservations of parents in keeping such young children in SAI hostels.

(iii) Under the Army Boys Sports Company (ABSC) Scheme, the age for admission has now been increased to 17-1/2 years, because talented sportspersons under this scheme are admitted virtually in the form of recruitment to the Army, for which there are minimum age related limits / limitations.

In addition to the SAI Scheme, there are various Schemes of the State Governments in the form of sports colleges and sports hostels, etc., also in which talented young sportspersons would be getting admission, but details in this regard are not available, and would have to be compiled.

The need here is to develop a system of talent spotting, in the context of the proposals for broad-basing sports, a major objective of which is also to significantly increase the catchment for spotting of talent which could be subsequently nurtured and trained. The twin measures required would pertain to the development of a system of spotting talent and provision of facilities where training could be given. In so far as the former is concerned, a major issue would pertain to the methodology and capacity building to spot talent early at the grass roots level in the context of the proposed Panchayat Yuva Khel Abhiyan Scheme (PYKA), and at other levels. The following measures would require to be taken in this background:

(a) SAI will develop a capacity building programme for organisers of competitions under PYKA for the purpose of training them in the field of talent spotting;

(b) For this purpose, retired sportspersons, physical education teachers/instructors and suitable ex-army/para-military personnel could also be identified and their involvement enlisted at the village and block levels;

(c) A pool of trained talent spotters would be created to identify talent during district and state level competitions, in addition to visits by SAI experts to various state academies/accredited centres of excellence periodically to identify hidden talents;

(d) The number of schools adopted under the NSTC scheme will need to be significantly increased and the intake in such schools also increased, wherever necessary and feasible;

(e) The operation of the scheme in the Navodaya Vidyalayas will be reviewed in consultation with the Ministry of Human Resource Development (HRD) with the aim of developing a system whereunder identified talented youngsters could be admitted as a separate category with a daily schedule focusing on their training and to adopt, if necessary, a separate curriculum based on open school examination system for them;

(f) Various adopted schools could concentrate on a particular discipline(s), depending on the local potential in the area; and

(g) Focused action will need to be taken to take care of the educational requirements of talented children admitted in various SAI Centres.

(h) The ABSC scheme run by SAI with Indian Army would also need to be linked with the talent spotting and competition structure from the sub-district up to the state level, so that identified talented persons at various levels could be suitably accommodated in the training structure of ABSC. This would significantly enhance the total number of trainees under the Scheme during the XIth Plan. In addition, similar schematic arrangements should be worked out with some of the Central Para-military forces.

The State governments would also need to take various measures, which are briefly outlined below :

(a) to prepare an integrated State level Annual Competition Calendar (incorporating events at village, block, district and state level);

(b) to build up a team of trained talent-spotters for identification of talent from village level competitions onwards, in coordination with SAI;

(c) to create appropriate sports infrastructure at district and state levels;

(d) to ensure availability of human resources for training and scientific/technical backup at district and state levels;

(e) to streamline their existing sports-schools, academies, training centres, etc. to take care of nurturing and training of identified talent at district and state levels;

(f) to synergise the efforts and resources of State Sports Associations, outstanding sportspersons, Corporate sector, SAI, etc. towards creation of requisite infrastructure and integrating it with the competition, talent spotting and training structures at district and state levels; and

(g) to create an integrated data-base of the talent identified at the state level for future planning and management.

The systematic interplay of properly established competition and talent spotting structures as brought out in the foregoing paragraphs would need to be synchronised with a parallel network of training centres / sports schools / centres of excellence/academies, with inputs based on a scientifically established profile of the trainees and targeted achievement levels.

Promotion of Sports Excellence

The broad-basing matrix outlined above could gradually yield, during XIth Plan, a vast pool of upto 100,000 talented youth at the Sub-Junior, Junior and Senior levels, who would require systematic and scientific nurturing and focused training, to achieve excellence at the national/international levels. This would require multiple measures, including spotting/identification of national probables based on proficiency, performance and potential, establishment of training infrastructure and arrangements for need based and integrated training, expanding and improving coaching facilities, strengthening scientific and technical supports systems, ensuring the availability of quality sports goods and equipments, use of media to bring sports consciousness, etc., to be taken during the XIth Plan.

National Sports Training Infrastructure Grid : The Working Group emphasized the need for developing a comprehensive national network of sports training facilities and infrastructure. It was observed that, so far, at the Central Government level, there has only been a focus on the infrastructure and facilities being developed by the Sports Authority of India, and no systematic action has been taken to map the facilities created by various

State Governments, private sector, etc. These not only comprise facilities set up by State Governments in the form of sports schools, hostels, academies, etc., but also infrastructure facilities for playing which would need to be linked with various aspects of training also. The following steps would have to be taken during the Eleventh Plan in this background :

i) Immediate action needs to be taken to develop a computerised data-base of all major sports infrastructure/training facilities established by different agencies in different parts of the country, and the manner in which they are being used;

ii) Further expansion of facilities by SAI should be undertaken keeping in view the facilities already available in different areas, which could be suitably utilised by them, and there should be focus, in the first instance, on completing/operationalising ongoing/sanctioned proposals;

iii) Specific steps should be taken by the Sports Authority of India to identify major sports facilities developed by the State Governments under various schemes, and with reference to specific events, like the National Games, Afro-Asian Games, Commonwealth Youth Games, World Military Games, etc., and work out arrangements for using these facilities for training, holding of coaching camps, etc.,

iv) Non-Governmental Organisations, outstanding sportspersons, and corporate entities should be encouraged to get involved in the creation of facilities to promote sports excellence, in the form of academies, etc.;

v) In the long run, a system of accreditation / ISO type Certification should also be evolved with reference to the quality of facilities available in, and operations of, institutions of excellence;

vi) While developing training facilities, optimization of resources should also be kept in view, for example, establishing playing surfaces for 6 - a side type of activities, and focus should also be given on specific elements of certain events/disciplines which require particular attention, for example Penalty Corner Conversion in the case of Hockey; and

vii) Wherever possible, the existing sports infrastructure should be used by schools and other educational institutions. This is particularly relevant in view of the rapidly shrinking availability of open spaces and play-grounds, specially in urban areas.

viii) In addition, efforts should also be made to develop revenue generating models with reference to the existing sports infrastructure so that maintenance requirements can be met to the extent possible.

Coaching:

It clearly emerged from the deliberations of the Working Group that the availability of well qualified coaches is a critical area for the promotion of sports excellence, and requires focused attention in the Indian context. It was also observed that there are different types of coaching requirements at different levels, and there are complexities associated with the process of selection; service conditions, performance appraisal and entitlements, etc., which would need to be addressed.

As regards the requirements at different levels, these could be broadly categorised as under:

(a) Basic level coaching and training, including talent spotting, at the grassroots levels (up to the district level) and in the school system;

(b) A proficiency based hierarchy of qualified and experienced coaches required under schemes of NSTC., STCs, SAG Centres, COX, State Academies, etc., to cater to the needs of identified groups/ categories of talented sportspersons at various levels; and

(c) Top class, International level/foreign coaches for specialised training of elite sportspersons / prospective international medal winners.

The strategy to be adopted in respect of each of these categories is briefly discussed / outlined in the following:

(i) The provision of coaches/trainers at the basic level would obviously have to be seen in terms of a mass requirement. In so far as the school system is concerned, this would need to be provided through the physical education teachers/instructors. The requirements at the village and block levels will have to be met largely through a semi-voluntary system, coupled with the aspect of capacity building, and involvement of other human resource elements.

(ii) As far as coaches in the second category, mentioned above, are concerned, the issues requiring attention and consideration would relate to numbers and requirement, level of qualification and competence, and aspects related to service conditions, career progression, etc. For purposes of this report, this would mainly concern the requirements of the SAI. As far as the total requirement is concerned, it was observed that there is presently a considerable shortage, since there has been no recruitment since 1991, and there is also an imbalance in terms of the availability of coaches for different disciplines. It will be necessary that SAI works out their overall requirements with respect to different disciplines, and draws up a phased programme for recruitment of coaches. The other aspects to be kept in view in this context are :

— While working out the requirement, provision could also be kept for a pool to meet special requirements of State Governments, and within the SAI system itself.

— Apart from direct recruitment, on a regular basis, appointment of coaches, on a contract basis, from among former/retired outstanding sportspersons/medal winners, should be considered. This could be accompanied by a short term capsule course in coaching for such persons. This would also create employment avenues for retired sportspersons.

— Outstanding sportspersons employed in Public/Private Sector Organisations, could be employed on secondment/deputation basis.

— Among directly recruited coaches, career progression, designations, and scales should, so far as possible, be based on stringently determined attainment of progressively higher levels of expertise through refresher/specialised courses, and performance (linked to established international norms and parameters, so far as possible), and there should be exit provisions linked to physical/medical fitness with a regular programme of physical tests, etc.

— Deployment and utilisation should be based on levels of expertise and actual requirements.

(iii) With reference to the third category, it was noted during the deliberations that, this would require a considerable degree of flexibility of approach, keeping in view the diverse nature of requirements, period of engagement, etc. This flexibility will also relate to levels of remuneration with reference to requirements of the Federations under the Scheme for financial assistance to NSFs, and the specific requirements of individual elite athletes/sportspersons. Keeping these aspects in view, it was felt that the possibility of bringing in some flexibility in the principles of funding/assistance to National Sports Federations (NSFs) should be explored, while the requirements of individual sportspersons could be met largely from the existing scheme of Talent Search and Training (to be suitably re-designated and revised) and the scheme of the National Sports Development Fund. This would be in addition to efforts to mobilise corporate sponsorship and support. This is also an area, where efforts should be made to derive maximum benefit from international cooperation programmes at a Government to Government level.

A general issue, which would also require attention pertains to the overall demand and supply situation with reference to coaches, which would need to be examined in depth and, if necessary, the capacity enhanced. In this context, the content of the courses and syllabi of the existing programmes of SAI/NIS Patiala would also need to be reviewed and brought in line with international standards and practices.

Scientific and Technical back-up / support

During the deliberations of the Working Group, it emerged that this area is of critical importance in the context of the current day competitive sports environment, and has not, so far, received the kind of attention that is required. This subject needs to be seen both in the context of its different constituent elements, and levels of provisioning. These are :

— The faculty level for purposes of the various academic programmes, pertaining to coaches, etc., being presently run by Sports Authority of India;

— Scientific and technical back-up and support with reference to various specialised disciplines (physiology, psychology, physiotherapy, etc.) during coaching camps, and for individual elite sportspersons;

— Technical back-up and support for teams/athletes participating in international competitive events;

— Very specific requirements of individual elite sportspersons; and

— Availability of high quality equipment in the major centres of training and sports excellence.

— On the technical side, it is also necessary to take concerted steps to develop a pool of highly qualified and accredited technical officials, such as judges, referees, etc.

So far, a scheme of Central Pool of Technical Equipments has been implemented by SAI. While this will need to be assiduously pursued, and availability of state-of-the-art equipments expanded, the ambit of planning and action will need to be widened to include the vital human resource elements as brought out above. In this context, an exercise would urgently need to be done to assess the overall requirements in the different categories mentioned earlier, identification of the elements which could be provided on the basis of outsourcing/ empanelment, etc., strict regulation by SAI and MoYAS with reference to the support personnel who accompany teams/contingents in international tournaments, etc. It is proposed to set up a Committee of experts to examine this whole issue in depth, so that further action could be taken in a planned manner.

In addition, special efforts would need to be made to develop a high class Sports Medicine and Rehabilitation Centre in the Country, with similar facilities at the Regional level. One option in this regard will be to identify suitable medical institutions/medical colleges, where such Centres could be developed by working in close coordination with the Institution/Department, as the case may be.

The aspect relating to Technical Officials is an area of considerable importance, not only with reference to the professional conduct of events within the country, but also with reference to safeguarding the interests of Indian sports and sportspersons at the international level. Concerted steps would, therefore, need to be taken, in this regard, in close coordination with National Sports Federations as a part of their Long Term Development Plans.

Scheme of Talent Search & Training: As mentioned earlier, this Scheme basically relates to promotion of excellence at the level of identified sportspersons who have already achieved a level of attainment. It is proposed to continue the Scheme with a revised scale of assistance, as the present amounts are not adequate keeping in view the international trends. The scheme is also proposed to be renamed as the "Scheme for Promotion of Excellence among high performing athletes". A suitable tracking and monitoring system will also have to be put in place.

National Sports Development Fund: As brought out in the review of the implementation of programmes during the Xth Plan, despite the fact that this is virtually the only scheme for institutionalised participation of the private/ corporate sector in the promotion of excellence in sports in diverse ways, their actual participation in the scheme has been negligible.

Also the diverse potentials of the scheme have not been effectively explored or realised. It emerged during the discussions that dissemination of information about the scheme is extremely inadequate, both among individual elite sportspersons and in the corporate world. Proactive measures will have to be taken to remove this deficiency, including large scale publicity. In addition, it was suggested that the level of fiscal benefits provided under the Scheme should be reviewed and made more liberal, which would need to be examined during the Eleventh Plan. In general, a very high priority and attention will need to be given to this scheme.

Scheme of State Sports Academy: This is another scheme, where mobilisation of private initiative, and establishment of a partnership between the State and Central Governments was sought to be achieved, in expanding and strengthening the infrastructure for promotion of excellence in sports. Though the aim was indeed laudable, no proposals have actually materialised.

It was felt during the deliberations that two diverse objectives were sought to be achieved through this scheme which may not necessarily be compatible viz. developing collaboration between the State and Central Governments, on the one hand, and developing Public-Private Partnership, on the other. In a sense, the former objective is already being sought to be achieved through the STC and SAG Centres Schemes of the SAI. The focus, therefore, needs to be on how to motivate and mobilise private participation and expertise in the establishment of such Academies.

In this context, it was also felt that the scope of the Scheme should be extended to cover proposals from Municipal bodies/Urban Development Authorities, Sports Clubs, Outstanding Sportspersons, Non-Governmental Organisations and the Corporate Sector, along with involvement and participation of SAI, and support could be extended in different ways which could, inter-alia, include the principle of viability gap funding. Guidelines and a basic framework for this purpose need to be worked out, on the basis of which, expressions of interest and specific proposals could be invited and further action on the same taken during the XIth Plan.

Emerging National Matrix: The systematic convergence and synergy between the programmes and various stakeholders associated with broad-basing and promotion of excellence as outlined above, would lead to a national framework comprising Competition.

In addition, an amount of Rs.1120 crores is proposed for Commonwealth Games 2010 which can be termed as a special scheme and, in that context should be viewed separately while looking at the step up in the outlays of Ministry's budget as compared to Xth Plan.

10

International Year of Sport and Physical Education

During the International Year of Sport and Physical Education 2005, an initiative of the Government of Tunisia, 70 countries worldwide appointed national focal points to coordinate commemorative events; in addition, 52 other countries reported on commemorative activities without having officially appointed national focal points. International conferences and consultations were organised by Governments, international, inter-governmental and non-governmental organisations (NGOs), and research institutes. Activities within the International Year's framework, many with the support of the United Nations system, aimed at following up on the recommendations of the Inter-Agency Task Force on Sport for Development and Peace in its report entitled Sport for Development and Peace: Towards Achieving the Millennium Development Goals, published in October 2003.

In achieving its objectives, the International Year built on the experience of the European Year of Education through Sport 2004. Although measuring the many dimensions of the success of the International Year is not easy.

Institutional Arrangements

The decision of the General Assembly to observe an international year dedicated to sport and physical education required institutional arrangements to support the ideals and objectives proclaimed by the international community. These arrangements consolidated and built on the many efforts undertaken prior to the year in support of these ideals and objectives, and, in particular, focused commemoration of the International Year on long-term action to establish the role of sport and physical education as a tool for development and peace.

Following the adoption of General Assembly resolution 58/5, Mr. Adolf Ogi, Special Adviser to the Secretary-General on Sport for Development and Peace, proposed to the Secretary-General the establishment of the United Nations Office for the International Year of Sport and Physical Education. The establishment of the Office was approved by the Secretary-General in December 2003 and it was set up in May 2004. No financial request was made to the United Nations for the establishment of the Office; rather, its success has been dependent on the determination and will of all partners involved, on the financial assistance of the Swiss Agency for Development and Cooperation, following the establishment of a trust fund by the United Nations Fund for International Partnerships (UNFIP), and on the support in kind of the United Nations Office at Geneva.

A core objective of the Office for the International Year was the global coordination of the commemoration of the Year and the promotion of sport as a partner for development and peace, contributing to the achievement of the MDGs. The Office worked in close cooperation with the Office of the Special Adviser to the Secretary-General on Sport for Development and Peace in Geneva. In October 2004, the United Nations New York Office of

Sport for Development and Peace was created with the support of the United Nations Development Programme (UNDP) to assist the Special Adviser to the Secretary-General on Sport for Development and Peace. The three offices worked together to advocate the power of sport in achieving identified goals and to facilitate and promote commemorative activities in connection with the Year.

The Working Group on Sport for Development and Peace of the United Nations Communications Group, under the leadership of the United Nations New York Office of Sport for Development and Peace, held regular meetings throughout 2005 among United Nations agencies and with other partners to maximise the impact of sport activities and programmes throughout the United Nations system, as detailed in its business plan. The Working Group helped promote commemorative activities for the International Year. A task force on resource mobilisation was created within the Working Group with the aim of encouraging non-traditional partners and donors to support policies and activities through field projects and partnership programmes.

National and Regional Stage

In accordance with the Economic and Social Council guidelines for the observance of international years, special attention was given to the role of Governments in the commemoration activities. Member States were invited by a note verbale from the Secretary-General to establish multi-stakeholder national committees or national focal points to plan, coordinate and implement national observance of the International Year. The valuable contribution of the United Nations Information Centres (UNICs) and the UNDP country offices in assisting in identification of a significant number of national focal points is recognised.

Action at the country level in coordinating and publicising commemorative activities is testimony to the success of the International Year and has ensured that a growing network of Governments, organisations, groups and individuals around the world are made aware of sport and physical education's vital role in contributing to education, health, development and peace. National focal points have been established in 70 countries. Beyond those countries which established national focal points, a further 52 countries have been particularly active in forwarding the objectives of the Year with reports on their activities made to the Office for the International Year.

All countries are encouraged to continue activities beyond 2005 to help develop and implement sustainable sporting and physical education programmes and policies designed to respond to the specific needs and conditions of their communities. The call for reporting on the International Year made by the Office for the International Year drew responses from many national focal points suggesting that national committees established for the Year had evolved - or were considering evolving - into permanent bodies.

It is beyond the scope of the present report to describe the multitude of events, activities and initiatives undertaken within the context of the International Year. Therefore, the following summary highlights the key areas of interest and priority themes, and presents a brief overview of activities held in various regions around the world during the Year.

Africa

Based on information provided to the Office of the Special Adviser to the Secretary-General on Sport for Development and Peace, 19 national focal points were appointed for observance of the International Year in

Africa, in the following countries: Burkina Faso, Cameroon, the Central African Republic, Chad, the Comoros, Eritrea, Ethiopia, Ghana, Malawi, Mauritania, Mauritius, Mozambique, Niger, Sao Tome and Principe, Senegal, Seychelles, Sierra Leone, South Africa, and Zambia.

Many projects were organised in partnership with United Nations agencies in various countries throughout the continent. For example, the United Nations Environment Programme (UNEP) organised nature and sports camps for children in slum areas in Nairobi. In Sierra Leone, a United Nations inter-agency sport pilot project proposal was formulated which called for the inclusion of sport-based elements into currently implemented development programmes.

Round tables and workshops were held in Burundi, Cameroon, Ethiopia, Mozambique, Niger and Nigeria. Following the Next Step II Conference in Zambia, the President of the Republic of Zambia announced the re-introduction of physical education into the mandatory school curriculum as a pillar to foster education, health and personal development.

Mass-participation running and walking races in Cameroon, the Comoros, Ghana, Kenya, Mali and Togo met their objectives of sensitising the population about the benefits of sport and physical activity for all.

Special events and festivals were held in Cameroon, Lesotho and Mauritius. Ghana adopted a slogan, "Sport For Life", and in Seychelles a national theme, "Our Children, Our Treasure, Our Future" was used in the context of the International Year. Sport was used as a tool in Liberia to raise awareness to help protect children from HIV/AIDS. In South Africa, the University of Pretoria adopted a declaration of support for the Year.

Many NGOs are active in Africa promoting sport and physical education as a tool for education, health, development and peace. As an example, Sport - The Bridge has been active in Ethiopia and established the "Ethiopia - Sport Builds Bridges" project for socialising street children in Addis Ababa. In Kenya, the Kenyan Community Foundation has undertaken a number of activities throughout the country. The following NGOs, Alive and Kicking Kenya, Play Soccer, Right To Play, and the Tegla Loroupe Peace Foundation have used sports as a mobilising tool to build trust among warring communities and promote public awareness.

Asia and the Pacific

Based on information provided to the Office of the Special Adviser to the Secretary-General on Sport for Development and Peace, 14 national focal points were appointed for observance of the International Year in Asia and the Pacific, in the following countries: Australia, Bhutan, Fiji, India, Mongolia, Nauru, New Zealand, the Philippines, Samoa, Sri Lanka, Thailand, Tonga, Tuvalu and Vanuatu.

Throughout the region numerous activities were undertaken in commemoration of the International Year including: a mass-participation run in India; an annual Push Play Day to celebrate and promote physical activity in New Zealand; a table tennis tournament with the theme "Sports for Health and Happiness" in Bhutan; and the Tour of Qinghai Lake International Road Cycling Race in China. In recognition of their efforts in overcoming regional tension and encouraging peaceful relations, the national cricket teams of India and Pakistan were appointed spokespersons for the Year.

Conferences commemorating the International Year were held in India, Malaysia, Pakistan and Samoa. Thailand hosted the International Conference on Sport and Education in Bangkok. The 2005 Arafura Games International Sport Conference "Celebrating Sport and Culture" was held in Darwin, Australia.

In reaction to the devastating tsunami of December 2004, the international sporting community held a number of activities rallying support, including round tables in Switzerland and Thailand.

Australia dedicated numerous public awareness-raising activities to the commemoration of the International Year, such as the Australian Youth Olympic Festival, and the Indigenous Sport and Recreation Program. The 2005 Australian University Games were the first official Australian sporting event to be endorsed by the United Nations for their role in instilling the values of fair play, peaceful competition and the pursuit of excellence.

Europe

Based on information provided to the Office of the Special Adviser to the Secretary-General on Sport for Development and Peace, 20 national focal points were appointed for observance of the International Year in Europe, in the following countries: Albania, Austria, Belarus, Bulgaria, Finland, France, Georgia, Germany, Greece, Latvia, the Netherlands, Norway, Poland, the Russian Federation, Spain, Sweden, Switzerland, The former Yugoslav Republic of Macedonia, Turkey and the United Kingdom of Great Britain and Northern Ireland.

With 2004 being the European Year of Education through Sport, activities commemorating the International Year of Sport and Physical Education tended to build on those already commenced, enabling consolidation of initiatives on sport as a tool for education, with additional initiatives also undertaken on sport for health, development and peace. Throughout

2005, contacts with the European Union continued, enabling evaluation and dissemination of best practices of European projects throughout the region.

A study by OXFAM GB found that the Indian Ocean tsunami had taken the life of four times as many women as men. Therefore, development projects such as Austria's "Women Swimming into the Future: promoting and strengthening women in the South Asian Tsunami region" were initiated. The Government of Ireland supported an "Active School Initiative", an initiative that was first introduced as part of the European Year of Education through Sport and is being continued during 2006 to create a link between the European Year and the International Year.

The European Parliament, in its resolution on sport and development adopted on 1 December 2005 welcomed the International Year and emphasized that sports projects can be a cross-cutting means of building capacity in education, health in general, HIV/AIDS prevention and peace-building and to combat social exclusion, violence, inequalities, racism and xenophobia.

A number of conferences took place throughout Europe in the framework of the International Year including: a round table on inclusion and sports participation in the European Union and the European Commission's Consultation Conference with the European Sport Movement on the Social Function of Sport, Volunteering in Sport and the Fight against Doping, in Belgium; the European Association for Sport Management's "Power of Sport Congress" in the United Kingdom; the XVIIth European Sports Conference, in Greece; a symposium on the meaning of sport science for the political decision-making process in Germany; "The EU and Sport: Matching Expectations", in Belgium; "The International Year of Sport and Physical Education" Congress in Spain; and "Cooperation of governmental and nongovernmental organisations in the field of 'Sport for All' development", in Serbia and Montenegro. The Conference of the Youth and Sports Ministers of French-speaking Countries and the first meeting of European government experts on the topic "Sport and disability", were held in France. The Church and Sport Section of the Holy See organised its first ever seminar on the theme "The Christian mission in the field of sport today".

Mass-participation sporting events were held in Albania, Belarus, Italy and the Russian Federation. Events linking sport with development and peace were held in Afghanistan, Azerbaijan, Bosnia and Herzegovina, Kazakhstan, Poland and Serbia and Montenegro. Charity football events were held during the year in Barcelona (Spain), Innsbruck (Austria) and Munich (Germany), and the 16th Vienna-Budapest Super Marathon was held under the theme "Run without borders".

Many European countries have been involved in sports and physical education projects that contribute to education, health, development and peace in developing countries. For example, the Finnish governmental organisation, LiiKe, has been involved with schools in the United Republic of Tanzania. France provided financial support to the NGO, Sport Sans Frontières (Sport without borders) to contribute to improving the situation of deprived children and women through sport and promoting national reconciliation in Afghanistan and Kosovo. UK Sport, together with the Norwegian Sports Confederation and National Olympic Committee, supported the Next Step II Conference in Zambia, and the Kicking AIDS Out! courses in Malawi. Austria used sport in development projects such as "Rwanda: kicking for reconciliation in Kigali".

In Switzerland, thousands of initiatives were undertaken to commemorate the International Year both within the country and around the world. Financial assistance facilitated the work of Mr. Adolf Ogi, Special Adviser to the Secretary-General on Sport for Development and Peace and former President of the Swiss Confederation. A National Committee composed of different federal offices and other institutions was formed to create nationally coordinated promotional programmes under the leadership and coordination of the Federal Office of Sport. Eight nationally coordinated promotional programmes were initiated including the "Schools on the move" project which made nearly 30,000 children from all over Switzerland physically active every day.

A "Constitutional Run" from district to district was held in Zurich. The Swiss Agency for Development and Cooperation, the Pestalozzi Children's Foundation (PCF) and the Office for the International Year of Sport and Physical Education 2005 hosted the International Youth "Play for Peace"-Camp. A working group was set up that supports sport and development projects worldwide.

Public-awareness initiatives and promotional activities took place throughout Europe. In commemoration of the International Year, a number of Internet platforms were established, inter alia, in Germany, the Netherlands, Norway, Poland, Portugal, the Russian Federation, Spain and Switzerland.

France disseminated information on United Nations activities and the objectives of the Year in booklets, posters, and advertisements. In Germany, the Ministry of Interior launched a public poster campaign about the Year, emphasizing that sport and physical activity are possible for all. Latvia's poster campaign was launched under the theme "Sport and education: one language". In Austria, projects were initiated such as "Female athletes as role models for girls and women".

A gymnastics and sports association team from Denmark toured 20 countries and widely disseminated documentation on the Year and the use of sport for education, health, development and peace. In Finland, in partnership with the Finnish United Nations Association and a number of NGOs, the UNDP Nordic Office organised the "Sauna Bus" Tour to promote the Year, the MDGs, and the United Nations sixtieth anniversary celebrations.

The United Kingdom is preparing a "Sport for Development" evaluation manual. The Netherlands held an extensive campaign with the Dutch governmental agency NCDO in collaboration with approximately 30 Dutch organisations to spread the message of the Year that reached around 2.5 million people in the Netherlands.

United Nations funds, programmes and specialised agencies collaborated with local partners to organise events using the International Year's logo in Albania, Armenia, Belarus and Bulgaria. With the support of the United Nations Mission in Kosovo, the Year proved an excellent platform from which to launch sport-based projects aimed at young people, contributing to a morre peaceffull sociietty.

Latin America and the Caribbean

Based on information provided to the Office of the Special Adviser to the Secretary-General on Sport for Development and Peace, eight national focal points were appointed for the International Year in Latin America and the Caribbean in the following countries: Bolivia, Brazil, Chile, Colombia, Cuba, Mexico, Paraguay and Trinidad and Tobago.

Brazil hosted the Latin American and Caribbean Youth Leadership Summit. Cuba hosted the World Convention on "Psycho Motor Function, Stimulation and Infants Health" and the "Latin-American Forum of Physical Education and School Sports Teachers".

The Trinidad and Tobago Alliance for Sport and Physical Education, in collaboration with other local and regional stakeholders, held several activities in commemoration of the International Year including an international sport and physical education convention; a mass-participation Jump Rope for Heart programme; and continuation of a Youth Empowerment through Sport programme. A commemorative music video was produced to promote the theme of the Year in the Caribbean.

During the International Year, activities in Argentina, Belize, Chile, Costa Rica and Mexiço focused on public-awareness activities, workshops and international forums. The Government of Brazil, through sport-based special programmes such as "Segundo Tempo" and "Pintando a Liberdade", sought to address deprivation and social problems. Currently, about one million people take part in the "Segundo Tempo" programme throughout Brazil.

The town of Medellín in Colombia hosted events including an international "Football for peace" tournament organised by the NGO, Streetfootballworld, and "26 hours of athletics" to celebrate sport's social contributions in offering alternatives for young people to risks such as violence, drugs and alcohol.

Middle East and North Africa

Based on information provided to the Office of the Special Adviser to the Secretary-General on Sport for Development and Peace, eight national focal points were appointed for the International Year in the Middle East and North Africa, in the following countries: Algeria, Bahrain, Israel, Lebanon, Morocco, Qatar, Tunisia and the United Arab Emirates.

As with other regions throughout the world, public-awareness activities concerning the International Year were evident in the Middle East and North Africa. Tunisia, as initiator of the Year, carried out an "Awareness Campaign" about the benefits of sport and physical education. The Government of Tunisia, with the support of UNDP, organised an international conference on sport and health, aimed at highlighting the critical role of sport in health promotion; the Arab Conference on Sport and Education; a Sport and Development Conference; and various events in connection with labour, education and youth.

Israel organised public-relations campaigns, including the distribution to all schools of posters with the official logo of the International Year and held "National Physical Education" weeks. Morocco organised activities under the slogan "Sport for all, together for a better world" and stamps were issued commemorating the Year. The Islamic Republic of Iran's sports radio channel broadcast comprehensive sport and health programmes making it one of the most successful radio channels in 2005. In Algeria, open days within sporting federations were organised to highlight sport and physical education.

Throughout the Middle East and North Africa, conferences and workshops were held publicising the United Nations objectives for the International Year. The Wingate Institute, Israel's National Center for Physical Education and Sport, hosted the Fourth Post-Olympic Conference. The Third West Asian Games 2005 were held in Qatar. Yemen successfully hosted the Third Asian Conference on Women and Sport. A conference on the value of sport in human development and a national seminar on women and sport were held in Oman. Morocco hosted the 68th Annual Congress of the International Sports Press Association, a workshop on the empowerment of sports educators, and the Second Pan-African Youth Leadership Summit that highlighted the power of sport in advancing health, education and development while promoting tolerance and peace.

Sport activities in Bahrain showed great improvement in 2005 due to the Government's willingness to increase significantly the budget for the development of sport and youth activities with six world-class sports championships hosted in Bahrain in 2005. In Egypt, the Islamic Republic of Iran and Kuwait, activities related to the International Year included workshops, games, national festivals and running events. The Islamic Republic of Iran National Olympic and Paralympics Academy carried out approximately 150 educational programmes in which 11,000 people participated. Advisers to the National Olympic Committee of Iraq have advocated for social responsibility and public diplomacy to be at the heart of the Committee's sport development strategy.

North America

In Canada, hundreds of special events and celebrations were held over the course of the International Year. A Canadian Year of Sport and Physical Education logo was developed, disseminated widely and integrated into promotional material, conference themes and special events. As a culminating event for the International Year, CAHPERD hosted a National Physical Education Forum, "Time to Listen/Time to Learn/Time to Act", in Ontario. Canada also hosted the 2005 Congress of the International Association of Physical Education and Sport for Girls and Women, "Learning to lead: women's influence on policy and practice in physical education and sport".

The United States of America hosted a number of major athletic events and a conference on gender and women in sports that helped forge constructive partnerships within the international community. The United States National Paralympic Academy hosted a biennial, two-day celebration of Paralympic sport for youth with physical disabilities.

The International Stage

United Nations activities and initiatives

The world of sport is a natural partner for the United Nations system and should be included in efforts to cultivate a "global partnership for development" - the eighth MDG. Sport provides an innovative avenue to engage civil society in development initiatives. United Nations organisations have used the International Year to highlight and encourage the use of sport in international development programmes and projects.

The United Nations New York Office of Sport for Development and Peace and the Working Group on Sport for Development and Peace of the United Nations Communications Group drafted a business plan that is intended to provide the United Nations system with a blueprint for promoting more systematic and coherent use of sport for development and peace activities, especially in conjunction with efforts to achieve the MDGs. To publicise and promote United Nations sport for development and peace activities and programmes, and in commemoration of International Year, the New York Office is producing a fortnightly electronic Sport Bulletin.

The Food and Agriculture Organisation of the United Nations (FAO) has been progressively strengthening its links with sporting events and personalities, as a means of increasing awareness of the issues of hunger and poverty among a wide audience, especially youth. A number of international sports personalities have been nominated as FAO Goodwill Ambassadors, who have been particularly instrumental in promoting the FAO TeleFood program during 2005.

The International Labour Organisation (ILO) is involved in local development and youth insertion through sport and training, particularly in El Salvador, Mozambique and Senegal. The ILO Youth Sport Program puts sport partners and sport values at the centre of a process that allows development and sports institutions to assess their needs and to pool efforts, resources and capacities in partnership to meet these needs.

The Joint United Nations Programme on HIV/AIDS (UNAIDS) has joined forces with the International Cricket Council with the primary aim of using cricket to raise public awareness of HIV and AIDS in the cricketplaying world, which accounts for some of the countries that are hardest hit by the epidemic.

In January 2005, the United Nations Children's Fund (UNICEF) hosted the first Global Workshop on the Monitoring and Evaluation of Sports for Development Programmes. At the FIFA Confederations Cup Germany 2005, UNICEF and FIFA engaged in a global communications campaign "With Children We Win", using football as a universal language to help bridge divides and promote core values for lasting peace, non-violence and tolerance. The UNICEF-FIFA campaign uses a football coaches' manual to help address the issue of violence and discrimination.

UNICEF and the Confederation of North, Central American and Caribbean Association Football signed a partnership pledge to benefit children in Latin America and the Caribbean. The International Olympic Committee, the Indian National Olympic Committee, UNICEF, UNAIDS and the International Federation of Red Cross and Red Crescent Societies (IFRC) jointly hosted a workshop on HIV/AIDS prevention through sport, encouraging partnerships at the local level between National Olympic Committees and UNICEF country offices focused on sports for development. Recognising the need for greater integration and collaboration around its approach to sports partnerships, UNICEF convened a strategic working group on sport to develop an integrated global framework on sport. In addition, with funds donated by Swatch, UNICEF and several partners expanded a national sports programme in Rwanda focused on HIV/AIDS and education.

The United Nations Department of Public Information (DPI) circulated information on the International Year to all United Nations agencies through the United Nations Communications Group and to the public through United Nations information centres worldwide. The DPI News and Media Division covers United Nations sport-related initiatives on the United Nations Web-based news service, the United Nations family audiovisual page and other outlets.

The Year was publicised by international broadcasters, and a French distributor, Tele Images International, promoted the Year in an animated series of 26 half-hour programmes on street football. The series was aired in over 100 countries around the world and its stories and characters were used in several products including books, comics, a DVD, a music single and album, clothes and bedding which convey the United Nations message about sport's values. These are to be released between February and June 2006.

Within the framework of the International Year, UNDP entered into a partnership with the NGO Right To Play agreeing to collaborate in three priority areas: (a) organisation and follow-up to the Sport for Development and Peace International Working Group; (b) knowledge sharing and exchange in the area of sport for development, with the objective to promote further the inclusion of sport for development in national development programmes and policies; and © exploration of future areas of cooperation in the area of sport for development. In further support of the work of the Working Group, UNDP accepted its chairmanship at the inaugural meeting in May 2005, and has actively participated in its work to date. UNDP has supported extensive programming activities throughout the Year across all regional groupings, including in Belarus, Chile, Finland, Indonesia, Timor-Leste and Ukraine.

During the International Year, UNEP played an active role in the Sport and Environment Commission of the International Olympic Committee and supported the Committee in organising regional seminars on sport and the environment in Dubai, Lusaka and Nairobi. An agreement was signed by UNEP and the Beijing Organising Committee of the XXIX Olympiad aimed at making the summer Olympics of 2008 environmentally friendly.

The United Nations Educational, Scientific and Cultural Organisation (UNESCO) played a key role in encouraging commemoration of the International Year. Several countries launched Global Action Weeks or special days, as a tool, for example, to promote traditional sports and games (Oman). Sport and physical education became a defined key component of quality education in Jamaica and Thailand. The educational dimension, health issues, scientific research and studies, doping, fair play and national programmes on sport and physical education were the core components of activities to which public authorities, development agencies, specialised agencies and sport and physical education staff unions and professionals dedicated their mobilisation efforts to raise awareness and advocate the key objectives of the Year. The unanimous adoption of the International Convention against Doping in Sport by the 33rd session of the UNESCO General Conference on 19 October 2005 is recognised as a significant achievement of the Year.

The United Nations Human Settlements Programme (UN-Habitat), through its municipal youth development programmes, has been working with sport and recreation organisations in slum areas to help inform young people about HIV/AIDS and reproductive health and to offer alternatives to drugs and crime.

As in the past ten years, the United Nations Office of the High Commissioner for Refugees (UNHCR) has continued to run sports activities in refugee camps, mostly in Africa, Asia and Eastern Europe, in partnership with sports-oriented donors such as the International Olympic Committee, Right To Play, Nike and the international volleyball, badminton and basketball federations, with a view to enabling UNHCR to expand its sports programmes further. Plans for a joint United Nations inter-agency pilot project in Sierra Leone are well under way. The Together for Girls project has been continued in Dadaab, Kenya, throughout the International Year using sports as a tool to promote female integration and retention in the educational system.

The United Nations Millennium Campaign reached out to sporting celebrities, associations and clubs in 2005 across all Campaign offices, most notably in Europe, where the FC Barcelona Foundation and Juventus Turin worked with the Campaign to promote the MDGs at a special football match on 24 August.

The United Nations Office on Drugs and Crime (UNODC) year-long campaign was launched on 23 June focusing on sports and health. The International Day against Drug Abuse and Illicit Trafficking, on 26 June, had the theme "Value yourself ... make healthy choices" and included involvement in sports.

Events in 2005 organised by the United Nations Programme on Youth offered opportunities for highlighting linkages between youth and sport for development and peace. Through consultative meetings and in response to a booklet entitled Making Commitments Matter: a Toolkit for young people to evaluate national youth policy, young people contributed to the ten-year review of the World Programme of Action for Youth.

The United Nations Volunteers (UNV) programme has recently been an operational partner in a project in Sri Lanka with the aim of boosting awareness of volunteerism and the MDGs and to foster cultural dialogue; on a volunteerism against violence project in collaboration with UN-Habitat and UNDP in Madagascar; and a project on youth and sports for development in refugee communities in Ghana. UNV will be one of the implementing partners in the joint United Nations inter-agency pilot project in Sierra Leone. In a speech at the launch of the Beijing 2008 Olympic Volunteer Programme in 2005, the UNV Executive Coordinator linked the spirit of the Olympics to that of volunteerism.

The World Health Organisation (WHO) undertook several normative projects, technical meetings and related activities directly linked to the International Year in cooperation with various partners at all levels. These actions, such as guidelines for physical activity policy and programme development and for promoting physical activity and sport for young people in and out of schools, are carried out in the context of WHO work in health promotion, integrated prevention/control of non-communicable diseases, implementation of the WHO Global Strategy on Diet, Physical Activity and Health, and achievement of the MDGs. Their implementation along with new ones will be pursued during the 2006-2007 biennium.

Major International Conferences and Events

Following the proclamation of the International Year, a number of international events were initiated to increase awareness of the value of sport and physical education for the promotion of the core themes of education, health, development and peace. The declarations that have emerged from over 20 international and 18 regional conferences organised within the framework of the International Year, reflect the firm conviction of the stakeholders involved in the importance of sport for a better world.

Sport and health: A major outcome of the International Year has been the adoption of the International Convention against Doping in Sport. This is the first time a legal instrument aimed at eradicating doping has been both binding and universal. The Hammamet Declaration adopted at the International Conference on Sport and Health in Tunisia reaffirmed the role of sport and physical education for the promotion of healthy and active lifestyles.

Sport and education: Participants at the International Conference on Sport and Education in Thailand agreed on the Bangkok Agenda for Action on Physical Education and Sport in School, in which Member States are encouraged to make it mandatory for every school to provide all students with adequate time for physical education and sport on a weekly basis.

Sport and development: An international workshop on sport for development was held at the end of 2004 in Switzerland. An International Conference on Sport and Urban Development was held in the Netherlands. The Next Step II Conference, "Taking sport for development home", in Zambia was attended by the BBC World Service Trust and resulted in a media event which reached over 20 million listeners across Africa.

The report of the United Nations Inter-Agency Task Force on Sport for Development and Peace clearly identified youth as one of the greatest beneficiaries of the effects of sport. Therefore, the United Nations New York Office of Sport for Development and Peace organised a Youth Leadership Summit series which highlighted sport as an entry point for mobilising youth to bolster efforts to achieve the MDGs and promote tolerance and peace. Pan-African, Pan-Asian, and Latin American and Caribbean Youth Leadership Summits were held, respectively, in Senegal, Morocco; Japan; and Brazil. The regional summits will culminate in a Global Youth Leadership Summit at United Nations Headquarters in New York from 30 October to 1 November 2006.

As a culmination of the International Year, the Swiss Agency for Development and Cooperation, the Swiss Federal Office of Sports and the Office of the Special Adviser to the Secretary-General on Sport for Development and Peace organised the 2nd Magglingen Conference on Sport and Development in Switzerland attended by over 400 participants from 70 countries. A Call to Action was adopted which led sport and development to the next stage emphasizing the need for global partnerships to be increased and strengthened. Partners at different levels will come together again in October 2008 in Magglingen, Switzerland, to share results and validate the impact.

Sport and peace: The use of sport as a means to promote intercultural, post-conflict and peacebuilding dialogues was highlighted at several international conferences and events particularly at the International Conference on Sport and Peace in the Russian Federation.

Sporting events commemorating the International Year were organised around the globe, including the first Islamic Solidarity Games; the Homeless World Cup 2005; the fifth Francophone Games; the Everest Peace Project;

and the International Wheelchair and Amputee Sports Federation World Games.

Various other international conferences on issues pertinent to the International Year were held in 2005 including: the fourth international world communication conference on sport and society, "Play the Game - Governance in Sport: The Good, the Bad and the Ugly" in Denmark; an International Conference on Sports and Development, in Norway; the International Forum Sports and Development: Economy, Culture, Ethics in Germany; "Celebrating Sport and Culture" in Darwin; an International Seminar on the Quality of Physical Education and Sport, in Benin; the "Sport and Joy" Conference in Italy; the SportAccord conference in Germany; and the 2nd World Summit on Physical Education in Switzerland.

Two major international summits on sport and the environment were held during the International Year, including the Sports Summit for the Environment, in Japan at which participants pledged to reduce pollution and enrich the natural environment so future generations might enjoy sports as they are enjoyed today, and the Sixth World Conference on Sport and Environment, in Kenya organised by the International Olympic Committee with the support of UNEP and held at UNEP headquarters.

The International Paralympic Committee hosted two Women in Sport Leadership Summits. Kennesaw State University, in the United States, and the ILO Universitas programme hosted the International Summit: Effecting Social Change Through Women's Leadership in Sport. The Summit addressed such topics as promoting gender equity, empowering women, and developing global partnerships related to education and sports. The conference outcome was a centre on social changes through women leadership in sports based at Kennesaw State University.

International Partnerships and Initiatives

Intergovernmental initiatives

At the 2005 World Summit held at United Nations Headquarters in New York in September, over 170 Heads of States and Government adopted General Assembly resolution 60/1 paragraph 145 of which underlines that sports can foster peace and development and can contribute to an atmosphere of tolerance and understanding, and encourages discussions in the Assembly for proposals leading to a plan of action on sport and development.

The Group of Friends of Sport for Development and Peace was initiated by the Government of Switzerland among permanent representatives to the United Nations in New York in January 2005. The Group serves as an intergovernmental platform aiming to encourage Member States to integrate sport actively into their international cooperation and development policies through the implementation of relevant United Nations resolutions and to work together with the different United Nations funds, programmes and specialised agencies, as well as with the Office for the International Year and the United Nations New York Office of Sport for Development and Peace. The Group is co-chaired by the Permanent Representatives of Switzerland and Tunisia, and includes representatives from Austria, Australia, Brazil, Canada, Chile, China, Germany, Greece, Italy, India, Mali, Norway, Pakistan, the Russian Federation, Senegal, South Africa, Thailand and the United Kingdom. The Group met regularly during 2005 and plans to expand its activities in 2006.

The Sport for Development and Peace International Working Group was announced by the NGO, Right To Play, at the 2004 summer Olympic Games in Athens, at a round table co-sponsored by UNFIP. Chaired by UNDP, the Working Group is supported by Government leaders, United Nations experts, Olympic athletes and sports federations, with the overall goal to contribute, through a set of recommendations, to systematic mainstreaming of sport into national and international development strategies and programmes. These recommendations will be presented at the 2008 Beijing Olympics, encouraging Governments to address the issue of sport for development and peace when formulating national and international development policies.

Governmental organisations for development and international cooperation

The outstanding role of governmental organisations in the field of development cooperation using sport and physical education as a tool for development and peace must be highlighted, particularly those in Austria, Brazil, Canada, Finland, Germany, the Netherlands, Norway, Switzerland and the United Kingdom. As a core group of similar entities, these organisations, through identification of needs in various countries around the world and the financing and organisation of projects and initiatives, have made a major contribution to the advancement of the objectives of the International Year.

Non-governmental organisations and the private sector

Several notable global initiatives and many existing projects and programmes received additional impetus as a result of the International Year, for example, ExChange for Peace, Fundación Defensores del Chaco, Global Sports Alliance, the International Sport and Culture Association, Kick Forward, Kicking AIDS Out!, Laureus, Magic Bus, the Mathare Youth Sports Association, Peres Center for Peace, Playing for Peace, Play Soccer, Red Deporte y Cooperación, Sports Coaches Outreach, Sport Sans Frontières, Streetfootballworld, Street League and Youth Charter, organisations which predominantly use street football as an educational tool in projects that promote self-esteem and intercultural understanding. Nike became the first in its industry to voluntarily disclose the names and locations of more than 700 active contract factories that currently make Nike-branded products worldwide in a publicly available Corporate Responsibility Report. The company intends to continue to use sport as a tool for positive social change. The NGO Right To Play has been using sport and play programmes to encourage the healthy physical, social and emotional development of the world's most disadvantaged children in partnership with United Nations agencies, Governments and sports federations and organisations.

Sports associations and federations

The International Year proved that international sports federations and organisations and the sport manufacturing industry are increasingly willing to become involved in humanitarian actions. Many federations provided reports on activities commemorating the Year indicating their contributions to humanitarian causes and the hosting of a number of seminars and events which have contributed to the validation and acceptance of sport and physical education as a tool in development work.

Partnership programmes were launched as an imperative step towards enabling a coordinated and coherent approach to the use of sport and physical education. In particular, sports federations, associations and organisations raised funds for natural disasters such as the Indian Ocean tsunami in 2004 and the earthquake in Pakistan in 2005.

The International Olympic Committee (IOC), which had already been instrumental in the proclamation of 1994 as the International Year of Sport and the Olympic Ideal when the Committee celebrated the hundredth anniversary of its creation, participated actively in developing activities for the commemoration of the International Year. In October 2005, the Committee and UNAIDS produced a toolkit for the sports community on HIV/AIDS awareness and prevention.

In 2005, FIFA established a Corporate Social Responsibility Department in recognition of the importance of being a socially responsible organisation. A celebrity football match was organised by FIFA in Barcelona to raise funds for victims of the tsunami. FIFA's short-term response for tsunami relief has included promoting play to help overcome trauma, and distributing equipment. Medium-term relief includes restarting football activities with financial support and long-term assistance includes the reconstruction and rebuilding of football structures and facilities. In 2005, UNICEF, FIFA and the South American Football Federation officially launched "Los chicos siempre ganan!" (Teenagers/adolescents always win!), intended to promote youth rights.

The President of the International Paralympic Committee signed a partnership agreement between the Committee and the Special Adviser to the Secretary-General on Sport for Development and Peace; the Committee hosted the International Paralympic Day in Bonn, Germany; and organised a Healthy Paralympians project in Rwanda, Uganda and the United Republic of Tansania. Significant contributions were made and support given in honour of the International Year by the

Committee to the article in the draft United Nations Convention on the Rights and Dignities of Persons with a Disability, which relates to the right to leisure, recreation and sports.

In the immediate follow-up to the International Year, the Secretary-General, the Special Adviser to the Secretary-General on Sport for Development and Peace, and the presidents of FIFA and the IOC attended the World Economic Forum in Davos, Switserland, at an event dedicated to sport for development and peace. For the first time, the World Economic Forum brought together leaders from the world of sport to discuss sport's role in improving the state of the world and to plan new initiatives. The Secretary-General and his Special Adviser also visited the headquarters of the IOC in Lausanne and FIFA in Zurich to discuss ways to strengthen collaboration.

Global Communications and Public-awareness Activities

The International Year was launched on 5 November 2004 at United Nations Headquarters in New York by the Secretary-General. At the event, the Special Adviser to the Secretary-General on Sport for Development and Peace named top-ranked tennis star Roger Federer and marathon champion Margaret Okayo, as spokespersons to promote the objectives of the Year. In 2005, the national cricket teams of India and Pakistan were also appointed spokespersons for the Year.

A number of United Nations funds, programmes and specialised agencies have worked successfully with the world of sport in the area of communications and awareness-raising on key issues through global and local efforts. A concept document including a CD-ROM, detailing the reasons behind the proclamation of 2005 as the International Year was published by the Office for the International Year.

Public information units of United Nations system organisations and DPI, in cooperation with various Governments and NGOs, advocated the International Year by distributing information and using its official logo during sports-related activities and events. Other countries provided a hyperlink from their sports ministry's website to that of the Year. These included Australia, Austria, Bhutan, Canada, Finland, Iraq, Trinidad and Tobago, Tunisia, and the United Kingdom. The Sport and Development International Platform website, financed by Switzerland, is dedicated entirely to sport and development.

The UNODC Global Youth Network, in cooperation with Right To Play issued a CD-ROM, a Coaches' Guide for Using Sport to Teach Healthy Life Skills which used the International Year logo and that of the UNODC 2005 campaign.

A brief introductory video in English was produced by a private sponsor and translated into three languages: Arabic, French and Spanish. Furthermore, the British Broadcasting Corporation (BBC), the International Volleyball Federation and UNHCR produced videos to increase further media outreach for the International Year.

An unprecedented amount of media attention was accorded to the issue of sport and physical education during the International Year. Globally, all forms of media provided impulsion and awareness to activities and initiatives commemorating the Year. A number of media interviews were held throughout the Year with a particular focus on the Swiss media.

Marketing tools were provided by the Swiss Committee for the International Year, with financing by the Swiss Agency for Development and Cooperation, in the form of stickers, flags, wrist warmers, caps and cushions.

A major product of the International Year has been the promotion and distribution of the international Toolkit Sport for Development available in CD-ROM or online. The Toolkit was a national initiative of the Netherlands Government-supported international development and cooperation agency NCDO, the Netherlands Olympic Committee and Ministry of Health, Welfare and Sport. From mid-September to mid-October, the International Paralympic Committee and Magnum Photos provided use of photos for an exhibition at the Palais des Nations in Geneva.

A number of research initiatives and publications were made during the International Year that have contributed to the consolidation of sport and physical education's role in education, health, development and peace, and that have enhanced understanding of the need for interdisciplinary research and information sharing to enable accountable monitoring and evaluation of projects to take place. Comprehensive reporting on sporting projects including the exchange of research results, approaches and experiences must continue.

Products from the United Kingdom included a paper published by UK Sport and the International Business Leaders Forum, Shared Goals: Sport and business in partnerships for development, aimed at encouraging the private sector to use sport in community projects for health and development; a paper that outlined how sport is now recognised as an important, powerful and under-exploited tool for development in post-conflict reconstruction; and a research tool, the Value of Sport Monitor. UK Sport and UNICEF have also commissioned the publication of a monitoring and evaluation manual for sport in development projects intended to contribute to increased organisational sustainability and programme effectiveness.

The International Paralympic Committee, the United Nations and the International Council of Sport Science and Physical Education (ICSSPE) promoted research on a number of topics concerned with sport for people living with a disability and the Paralympic Movement. ICSSPE published the sixth volume of its book series, Perspectives, on the topic of Health Enhancing Physical Activity. It explains why physical activity is important for public health, what kind and how much physical activity provides health benefits, and how to change physical activity behaviour.

The Swiss Agency for Development and Cooperation published a book, Sport for Development and Peace, providing an overview of the main themes, demonstrating opportunities and limitations, and outlining possibilities for future endeavours. ILO research has examined how youth leadership and skills development can be fostered through sports. ILO will publish a book on these findings entitled Beyond the Scoreboard in April 2006. The University of Basel, Switzerland, published International Comparison of Physical Education: Concepts, Problems, Prospects in recognition of the fact that in recent years, school physical education has been confronted with serious challenges in a large number of countries and regions.

Achievements

In accordance with Economic and Social Council resolution 1980/67, the International Year contributed to a better understanding of the value of sport and physical education for human development and a more systematic use of sport in development programmes. Evaluation of the Year shows that activities generated during 2005 are in many instances to be integrated into regular programmes. There has been awareness-raising about the benefits of sport and physical education in social and educational programmes, consciousness-raising campaigns and endeavours strengthened with concrete actions. Actors have been involved who had not participated prior to the Year.

The International Year provided a unique opportunity to use the convening power of sport to capture the attention of and mobilise individuals, organisations, communities and the public at large. It facilitated delivery of messages and programmes to a wide range of people at local, national, regional and global levels, drawing diverse groups together in a positive and supportive environment.

The perception of "sport" by the general public and at the Government level was expanded, emphasizing the notion of "sport for all". Programmes promoting sport for development and peace have gained greater attention and resources from Governments, civil society and private-sector partners globally.

The International Year illustrated the importance of sport and physical education for quality education and brought to light that physical education is continuously losing ground in formal education systems and that it is imperative that young people gain an appreciation of sport at school in order to ensure lifelong active and healthy living.

The private sector in the form of sports organisations, federations and providers of sporting goods has embraced the multi-stakeholder approach advocated during the International Year. Private-public partnerships have been established with United Nations agencies and increased information sharing has been enabled at all levels.

11

International Charter of Physical Education and Sport

PREAMBLE

The General Conference of the United Nations Educational, Scientific and Cultural Organization, meeting in Paris at its twentieth session, this twenty-first day of November 1978.

Recalling that in the United Nations Charter the peoples proclaimed their faith in fundamental human rights and in the dignity and worth of the human person and affirmed their determination to promote social progress and better standards of life,

Recalling that by the terms of the Universal Declaration of Human Rights everyone is entitled to all the rights and freedoms set forth therein without discrimination of any kind as to race, colour, sex, language, religion, political or other opinion, national or social origin, property, birth or other consideration,

Convinced that one of the essential conditions for the effective exercise of human rights is that everyone should be free to develop and preserve his or her physical, intellectual and moral powers, and that access to physical education and sport should consequently be assured and guaranteed for all human beings,

Convinced that to preserve and develop the physical. intellectual and moral powers of the human being improves the quality of life at the national and the international levels,

Believing that physical education and sport should make a more effective contribution to the inculcation of fundamental human values underlying the full development of peoples,

Stressing accordingly that physical education and sport should seek to promote closer communion between peoples and between individuals. together with disinterested emulation. solidarity and fraternity, mutual respect and understanding, and full respect for the integrity and dignity of human beings,

Considering that responsibilities and obligations are incumbent upon the industrialized countries and the developing countries alike for reducing the disparity which continues to exist between them in respect of free and universal access to physical education and sport,

Considering that to integrate physical education and sport in the natural environment is to enrich them and to inspire respect of the earth's resources and a concern to conserve them and use them for the greater good of humanity as a whole,

Taking into account the diversity of the forms of training and education existing in the world, but noting that, notwithstanding the differences between national sports structures, it is clearly evident that physical education and sport are not confined to physical well-being and health but also contribute to the full and well-balanced development of the human being,

Taking into account, furthermore, the enormous efforts that have to be made before the right to physical education and sport can become a reality for all human beings,

Stressing the importance for peace and friendship among peoples of co-operation between the international governmental and non-governmental organizations responsible for physical education and sport,

Proclaims this International Charter for the purpose of placing the development of physical education and sport at the service of human progress, promoting their development, and urging governments, competent non-governmental organizations, educators, families and individuals themselves to be guided thereby, to disseminate it and to put it into practice.

Article 1. The practice of physical education and sport is a fundamental right for all

1.1. Every human being has a fundamental right of access to physical education and sport, which are essential for the full development of his personality. The freedom to develop physical, intellectual and moral powers through physical education and sport must be guaranteed both within the educational system and in other aspects of social life.

1.2. Everyone must have full opportunities, in accordance with his national tradition of sport, for practising physical education and sport. developing his physical fitness and attaining a level of achievement in sport which corresponds to his gifts.

1.3. Special opportunities must be made available for young people, including children of pre-school age, for the aged and for the handicapped to develop their personalities to the full through physical education and sport programmes suited to their requirements.

Article 2. Physical education and sport for an essential element of lifelong education in the overall education system

2.1. Physical education and sport, as an essential dimension of education and culture, must develop the abilities, will-power and self-discipline of every human being as a fully integrated member of society. The continuity of physical activity and the practice of sports must be ensured throughout life by means of a global, lifelong and democratized education.

2.2. At the individual level, physical education and sport contribute to the maintenance and improvement of health, provide a wholesome leisure-time occupation and enable man to overcome the drawbacks of modern living. At the community level, they enrich social relations and develop fair play. which is essential not only to sport itself but also to life in society.

2.3. Every overall education system must assign the requisite place and importance to physical education and sport in order to establish a balance and strengthen links between physical activities and other components of education.

Article 3. Physical education and sport programmes must meet individual and social needs

3.1. Physical education and sport programmes must be designed to suit the requirements and personal characteristics of those practising them, as well as the institutional, cultural, socio-economic and climatic conditions of each country. They must give priority to the requirements of disadvantaged groups in society.

3.2. In the process of education in general, physical education and sport programmes must, by virtue of both their content and their timetables, help to create habits and behaviour patterns conducive to full development of the human person.

3.3. Even when it has spectacular features, competitive sport must always be in accordance with the Olympic ideal to serve the purpose of educational sport, of which it represents the crowning epitome. It must in no way be influenced by profit-seeking commercial interests.

Article 4. Teaching, coaching and administration of physical education and sport should be performed by qualified personnel

4.1. All personnel who assume professional responsibility for physical education and sport must have appropriate qualifications and training. They must be carefully selected in sufficient numbers and given preliminary as well as further training to ensure that they reach adequate levels of specialization.

4.2. Voluntary personnel, given appropriate training and supervision, can make an invaluable contribution to the comprehensive development of sport and encourage the participation of the population in the practice and organization of physical and sport activities.

4.3. Appropriate structures must be established for the training of personnel for physical education and sport. Personnel who have received such training must be given a status in keeping with the duties they perform.

Article 5. Adequate facilities and equipment are essential to physical education and sport

5.1. Adequate and sufficient facilities and equipment most be provided and installed to meet the needs of intensive and safe participation in both in-school and out-of-school programmes concerning physical education and sport.

5.2. It is incumbent on governments, public authorities, schools and appropriate private agencies, at all levels to join forces and plan together so as to provide and make optimum use of installations, facilities and equipment for physical education and sport.

5.3. It is essential that plans for rural and urban development include provision for longterm needs in the matter of installations, facilities and equipment for physical education and sport, taking into account the opportunities offered by the natural environment.

Article 6. Research and evaluation are indispensable components of the development of physical education and sport

6.1. Research and evaluation in physical education and sport should make for the progress of all forms of sport and help to bring about an improvement in the health and safety of participants as well as in training methods and organization and management procedures. The education system will thereby benefit from innovations calculated to develop better teaching methods and standards of performance.

6.2. Scientific research, whose social implications in this sphere should not be overlooked, must be oriented in such a way that it does not allow of improper applications to Physical education and sport.

Article 7. Protection of the ethical and moral values of physical education and sport must be a constant concern for all

7.1. Top-class sport and sport practised by all must be protected against any abuse. The serious dangers with which phenomena such as violence, doping and commercial excesses threaten its moral values, image and prestige pervert its very nature and change its educative and health promoting function. The public authorities, voluntary sports associations, specialized non-governmental organizations, the Olympic Movement, educators, parents, supporters' clubs, trainers, sports managers and the athletes themselves must combine their efforts in order to eliminate these evils. The media have a special role to play, in keeping with Article 8 in supporting and disseminating information about these efforts.

7.2. A prominent place must be assigned in curricula to educational activities based on the values of sport and the consequences of the interactions between sport, society and culture.

7.3. It is important that all sports authorities and sportsmen and women be conscious of the risks to athletes, and more especially to children, of precocious and inappropriate training and psychological pressures of every kind.

7.4. No effort must be spared to highlight the harmful affects of doping, which is both injurious to health and contrary to the sporting ethic, or to protect the physical and mental health of athletes, the virtues of fair play and competition, the integrity of the sporting community and the rights of people participating in it at any level whatsoever. It is crucial that the fight against doping should win the support of national and international authorities at various levels, and of parents, educators, the medical profession, the media, trainers, sports managers, and the athletes themselves, to ensure that they abide by the principles set out in the existing texts, and more particularly the International Olympic Charter against Doping in Sport. To that end, a harmonized and concerted policy must guide them in the preparation and application of anti-doping measures and of the educational action to be undertaken.

Article 8. Information and documentation help to promote physical education and sport

8.1. The collection, provision and dissemination of information and documentation on physical education and sport constitute a major necessity. In particular, there is a need to circulate information on the results of research and evaluation studies concerning programmes, experiments and activities.

Article 9. The mass media should exert a positive influence on physical education and sport

9.1. Without prejudice to the right of freedom of information, it is essential that everyone involved in the mass media be fully conscious of his responsibilities having regard to the social importance, the humanistic purpose and the moral values embodied in physical education and sport.

9.2. Relations between those involved in the mass media and specialists in physical education and sport must be close and based on mutual confidence in order and sport and to ensure objective and well-founded information. Training of personnel for the media may include elements relating to physical education and sport.

Article 10. National institutions play a major role in physical education and sport

10.1. It is essential that public authorities at all levels and specialized non-governmental bodies encourage those physical education and sport activities whose educational value is most evident. Their action shall consist in enforcing legislation and regulations, providing material assistance and adopting all other measures of encouragement. stimulation and control. The public authorities will also ensure that such fiscal measures are adopted as may encourage these activities.

10.2. It is incumbent on all institutions responsible for physical education .and sport to promote a consistent, overall and decentralized plan of action in the framework of lifelong education so as to allow for continuity and co-ordination between compulsory physical activities and those practised freely and spontaneously.

Article 11. International co-operation is a prerequisite for the universal and well-balanced promotion of physical education and sport

11.1. It is essential that States and those international and regional intergovernmental and non-governmental organizations in which interested countries are represented and which are responsible for physical education and sport give physical education and sport greater prominence in international bilateral and multilateral co-operation.

11.2. International co-operation must be prompted by wholly disinterested motives in order to promote and stimulate endogenous development in this field.

11.3. Through co-operation and the pursuit of mutual interests in the universal language of physical education and sport, all peoples will contribute to the preservation of lasting peace, mutual respect and friendship and will thus create a propitious climate for solving international problems. Close collaboration between all interested national and international governmental and non-governmental agencies, based on respect for the specific competence of each, will necessarily encourage the development of physical education and sport throughout the world.

Bibliography

Allen, N., "A case study of a successful health advocate program", *Journal of American College Health, 41*(6), 293-295, 1993.

Bandura, A., *Social foundation of thought and action: A social cognitive theory,* Englewood Cliffs, NJ: Prentice-Hall, 1986.

Basen-Engquist, K., "Evaluation of a theory-based HIV prevention intervention for college students", *AIDS Education and Prevention, 6*(5), 412-424, 1994.

Berkowitz, A.D., "From reactive to proactive prevention: Promoting an ecology of health on campus", In P.C. Rivers & E.R. Shore (Eds.), *Substance abuse on campus: A handbook for college and university personnel* (pp. 119-139). Westport, CT: Greenwood Press, 1997.

Buchanan, D.R., "How teens think about drugs: Insights from moral reasoning and social bonding theory", *International Quarterly of Community Health Education, 11*(4), 315-332, 1991.

Canterbury, R.J., Gressard, C.F., Vieweg, W.V., Grossman, S.J., McKelway, R.B., & Westerman, P.S., "Risk-taking behavior of college students and social forces", *American Journal of Drug Alcohol Abuse, 18*(2), 213-222, 1992.

Caron, S.L., "Athletes as rape awareness educators: Athletes for sexual responsibility", *Journal of American College Health, 41*(6), 275-276, 1993.

de Vries, H., Weijts, W., Dijkstra, M., & Kok, G., "The utilization of qualitative and quantitative data for health education program planning, implementation, evaluation: A spiral approach", *Health Education Quarterly, 19*(1), 101-115, 1992.

Green, L.W., & Kreuter, M.W., *Health promotion planning, an educational and environmental approach,* Mountain View, CA: Mayfield, 1991.

Grossman, S., Canterbury, R.J., Lloyd, E., & McDowell, M., "A model approach to peer-based alcohol and other drug prevention in a college population", *Journal of Alcohol and Drug Education, 39*(2), 50-61, 1994.

Kerr, D.L., & Gascoigne, J.L., "Getting to know generation X: Health education for the thirteenth generation", *Journal of Health Education, 27*(5), 268-273.

O'Leary, A., Goodhart, F., Jemmont, L.S., Boccher-Lattimore, D., "Predictors of safer sex on the college campus: A social cognitive theory analysis", *Journal of American College Health, 40*(6), 254-263, 1992.

Parcel, G.S. & Baranowski, T., "Social learning theory and health education", *Health Education, 12*(3), 14-18, 1981.

Perkins, H.W., "College student misperceptions of alcohol and other drug norms among peers: Exploring causes, consequences, and implications for prevention programs", In *Designing alcohol and other drug prevention programs in higher education* (pp. 107-206). Newton, MA: The Higher Education Center for Alcohol and Other Drug Prevention, 1997.

Index